The Share of Wages in the National Income
An Enquiry into the Theory of Distribution

L.S.E. research monographs

This series is published jointly with the London School of Economics and Political Science. It aims to make available research of originality and quality from the whole range of the social sciences, including all the fields and disciplines which are studied at the School. The intention is to provide a continuing outlet for serious scholarly work, and relatively quick publication. The books will be of interest to specialists in the various fields, irrespective of whether they are in universities, government departments, industries or elsewhere, as well as to libraries throughout the world.
The following monographs have already been published:

The Politics of Decontrol of Industry: Britain and the United States
Susan Armitage

Students in Conflict
Tessa Blackstone, Kathleen Gales, Roger Hadley, Wyn Lewis

The Business of Banking, 1891–1914
C.A.E. Goodhart

Criminal Responsibility
F.G. Jacobs

The Nineteenth Century Foreign Office: An Administrative History
Ray Jones

The Criminal Liability of Corporations in English Law
L.H. Leigh

The Theory of Customs Unions: A General Equilibrium Analysis
Richard G. Lipsey

Changes in Subject Choice at School and University
Celia M. Phillips

Russian Police Trade Unionism: Experiment or Provocation?
Dimitry Pospielovsky

Industrial Demand for water: a Study of South-East England
Judith Rees

The Administrative Functions of the French Conseil d'Etat
Margherita Rendel

Transporting Goods by Road: Policies, Techniques and Distribution Efficiency
Michael Webb

The Share of Wages in the National Income

An Enquiry into the Theory of Distribution

F. H. Hahn

London School of Economics and Political Science

Weidenfeld and Nicolson
5 Winsley Street London W.1.

ISBN 0 297 99451 4

Printed in Great Britain by
Redwood Press Limited
Trowbridge, Wiltshire.

Contents

Preface

To publish unchanged a thesis* written over twenty years ago is a dubious enterprise and certainly requires some explanation. This is particularly so when, as in this case, the author was too unsure of its worth to accept a publication offer made shortly after its completion.

A succinct explanation can be given straight away. But I want to use this opportunity for a rather more wide ranging and more polemical discussion of the kind of theory advanced in this book from the viewpoint of the present. In the course of this I hope that it may become clearer why I am offering this old wine now.

The brief explanation is this. The book is largely concerned with an exploration of the consequences for the theory of distribution of a postulated difference in the savings propensities out of wages and profits. This avenue of exploration has been much discussed in recent years and is often regarded as an alternative to older and in particular neo-classical theories. My approach was different: I believed that these macro-economic forces working on the shares in income would only be of real interest in the study of disequilibrium, which I took to be the 'normal' state of a capitalist economy. Thus while I derived formulae for the share of wages in a golden age (p. 78), I regarded them as basically uninteresting and concentrated my main attention on the study of cycles, non-steady growth and short-run equilibrium. The reason was, and is, the belief that in the description of a thorough-going equilibrium the requirement that no economic agent in such a state has any inducement to change his strategy, leads to conditions which have nothing to do with differential savings propensities and which must bear almost all the weight in a study of equilibrium shares. This will be clarified below. But the summary explanation of this enterprise is now complete: I was interested in a macro-theory of distribution using tools that have recently been used but for a different purpose and with a different stance *vis a vis* my predecessors. To that

* The first three months of my research were under the supervision of Professor Kaldor, the rest with Lord Robbins. Professor Kaldor recalls a conversation with me about 1947 in which he expressed the view that 'the best approach to distribution theory is macro-economic'.

extent it may turn out to be of current interest.

I now turn to a more detailed analysis.

I

I want to start with the muddle we have got into in recent years. For this purpose I call a theory of distribution neo-classical if it employs a model of perfect competition in permanent equilibrium. In chapter 1 it is called the production theory of distribution. This theory has nothing simple to offer in answer to the question why is the share of wages, or of profits, what it is? The question is prompted by our interest in the distribution of income between social classes, and social class is not an explanatory variable of neo-classical theory. The latter is not formulated in terms of workers and capitalists but in terms of inputs and outputs. This lack of contact between the economic theory and sociological reality may well be the most damaging criticism of the neo-classical construction. The underlying assumption of very many agents means that problems of economic power can be ignored and the relation of economic to sociological phenomena is also untreated, both of which, for instance, are notable features of Marxian economics. Much of the muddle we have been in stems from this. On the one hand, neo-classical practitioners have not been able to resist the temptation to make the theory yield simple answers to sociologically motivated questions. On the other hand economists impressed by the inadequacy of the model for such questions, instead of concentrating on its mechanical and too abstract formulations, have criticised it on logical grounds where, as it happens, it is particularly robust.

To make matters worse the controversy has been overlaid by ideological clap-trap: the neo-classical theorist is said to be justifying the status quo while his opponent is the harbinger of progress. This makes good after-dinner conversation, but hinders serious discussion and study. As for myself, if the world really resembled the neo-classical world, I would regard the world as singularly unjust and repulsive. But if the resemblance were really there, then it would be there, and as far as an economist is concerned that is the end of that.

The thing to do is to get the purely technical argument right. I start with a quotation from Dennis Robertson:

> 'The second class of objection is based on the misapprehension that the orthodox theory asserts that wages are *determined* by marginal productivity. It does not – it asserts that they *measure* it, and that there is

therefore a functional relationship between the rate of wages paid and the number of persons employed.'[1]

The misapprehension Robertson talks of is with us still and stems, one suspects, from the difficulty many experience in understanding that an equilibrium theory in general and the neo-classical theory in particular has nothing causal to say. Such a theory cannot 'tell us anything about the history of the world we live in'.[2] Prices and input-output combinations are said to be equilibrium prices and equilibrium input-output combinations if, when they rule, no economic agent has any inducement to change his method of production and no input or output is in excess demand. This in turn means that the maximum price an agent is willing to pay for a little more of an input, given the equilibrium prices, cannot exceed the equilibrium price of that input and the maximum price he would be willing to pay to retain the marginal unit of an input cannot be less than the equilibrium price of that input. In that sense the equilibrium price measures the marginal product of that input and this is a simple and logically indisputable feature of the construction.

When I wrote, this theory had not yet been properly and formally developed to take account of the time element of production, although of course there was the unsatisfactory Böhm-Bawerkian work and the over-aggregated extensions by Wicksell and others. Hence I frequently argued that the theory is best taken as applying to stationary states although in doing so I had it also in mind that it is bound to ignore important phenomena of uncertainty and innovations of an actual economy. This I still take to be so, but as far as the formal and abstract construction is concerned one can do a good deal better in 1971 than in 1951.

The present formal theory is the theory of intertemporarily efficient paths and their price duals. It is proper, on the present occasion, to ignore the special technical difficulties which arise because these paths extend into the indefinite future. To every efficient path, ignoring these difficulties, there corresponds a sequence of prices so that each production agent for his plan maximises the value of his profits at these prices. Note that all future inputs and outputs enter into these calculations. The marginal product interpretation of these prices for each agent is the same as before. In general there are many efficient paths. But while the economy produces some goods in order to use them in the production of others it also produces goods to consume. One is interested only in paths which are consumption efficient. (One cannot have more of some consumption good at any time without having less of some consumption good at that or other times.) There are again many of these. The system is 'closed' when we have chosen one of the consumption efficient plans.

Since one can show, ignoring the exceptions which arise because of the infinite duration of the economy, that every economy in intertemporal equilibrium is consumption-efficient, the efficiency interpretation of the equilibrium prices is valid. It is important to understand that the description of an equilibrium requires equations describing the equilibrium of producers (profit maximisation), and also a theory of choice of consumption. The theory is complete and rather beautiful.

A special case, much discussed of late, arises when one studies intertemporal equilibria in which the composition of output and relative prices remain constant through time – the balanced growth path. For this purpose one considers a constant returns to scale technology. Such a path is often discussed in the context of a special consumption assumption of the type used in this book. When prices are constant and a numeraire has been chosen, then the relation between the present price of present goods and the present price of future goods defines an interest rate which in the context of a perfect competition model it would seem natural to identify with the rate of profit. This however has been the source of much controversy and muddle.

It is rather easy to show the following. Take a producer in the steady state equilibrium described. Ask him what would be the maximum interest rate he would be willing to pay for the loan of one unit of numeraire which at the going prices he can spend on productive inputs as he likes. Then his answer cannot be an interest rate higher than the one ruling. Similarly he will not be willing to lend one unit of numeraire at an interest rate below the one ruling. How does he arrive at his answer? He calculates the increase in his maximum profit from spending one unit more or less of numeraire efficiently and calculates the equivalent annuity. In that sense then does the rate of interest measure the marginal return of investment at equilibrium prices. It is not *determined* by this return, it *measures* it.

But people have wanted to say more than this: they want to claim that the rate of interest measures also the social rate of return to the economy as a whole. Sometimes this can be demonstrated, and I refer the reader to a splendid paper by Bliss and Solow's fine book on this whole matter.[3] To pursue it would not only take me too far afield but would also be unnecessary. For as far as the neo-classical theory of distribution is concerned all we need to do is to find relative prices, quantities and the interest rate in steady state and be allowed to give the private marginal product interpretation. This the theory accomplishes.

Yet simple and straightforward as it all is it has given rise to one of the most useless controversies of recent years. For instance it has been claimed that the whole argument is 'circular', for how can the producer calculate his most efficient use of another unit of numeraire if he does not already know the interest rate, in which case how can his calculation be said to 'determine' the interest rate? It is the old confusion of which Robertson speaks. We are not asking that the producer should determine the interest rate. We are checking whether the interest rate we observe is an equilibrium interest rate and in the process find an interpretation for it. In general, what determines the interest rate, and incidentally it need not be unique, are all the equilibrium equations simultaneously. That is the neo-classical ones describing that each production agent chose amongst his inputs and outputs the most profitable combination and the equations describing consumption.

Sometimes it is claimed that the marginal productivity calculation is tautologous and hence useless. This is a non sequitur. It is true that the marginal productivity formulation is only a restatement of the requirement that at the going prices and interest rate profits should be maximised – but it is an interesting restatement. It is never claimed that the restatement produces new equations.

Lastly, it is often maintained that the system I have described is one equation short and 'cannot determine the rate of profit'. This is simply false. The neo-classical theory is not inherently short of equations although of course this in itself does not guarantee a solution.

From the point of view of this book it may be instructive to consider the special case of classical savings, which in a different context I discuss in Chapter 7. We may also at the same time face the problem that a neo-classical equilibrium is in general a full employment equilibrium.

Suppose that we are somehow told the rate at which, in any balanced path, producers are willing to accumulate durable inputs. Certainly that rate must not be larger than the rate at which non-produced inputs such as labour can be taken to grow; it may however be less. From the point of view of the theory, supposing homogeneous labour to be the only non-produced input, it is formally easiest simply to proceed *as if* the rate of growth of labour were the same as the given accumulation rate. One can then later compare the actual, with this hypothetical growth rate of labour to determine how unemployment will behave. One has dropped the requirement that the actual labour market be cleared at each moment of time. At the equilibrium wage no producer will want more labour than he has and the fact that there is unemployed labour seeking employment is taken as not inconsistent with equilibrium.

Now let us state and count equations and unknowns for the general case. Assume that there are (n – 1) producer goods, one consumption good and labour.

There will be n neo-classical equations demanding that profits be maximised. Since there are constant returns to scale, these equations depend only on prices and the rate of profit. Choose labour as the numeraire and verify that there are (n + 1) unknowns in these equations. For every rate of profit in a given range these equations can be solved for the n prices. But when they are solved they also tell us what techniques of production are chosen at each such rate of profit. Given the way households spend on consumption (i.e. the savings assumption) for any set of intensities with which the activities are used we will at a given rate of profit (and hence prices), be able to read off the wage and interest income of households and hence their consumption demand, and hence the demand for any good. However we require the output of every good to grow at the same rate which is given from outside the system. There is no reason to suppose that for the, at present, arbitrarily chosen profit rate, this is consistent with all markets being cleared. In other words we may at that profit rate be unable to find a combination of intensities with which the activities are used such that outputs grow at a given rate and all markets are in equilibrium. But one can show that to each profit rate there corresponds a growth rate, although not necessarily the given one, at which balanced growth is possible. Let n(r,p) be this growth rate expressed as a function of the profit rate r and the vector of prices, p. Let g be the given growth rate. Then one has the further equilibrium condition $g = n(r,p)$. This closes the system although one requires some technicalities to show that at least one solution exists.

In the special case in which we are interested where nothing is saved out of wages, this last equation reduces to $g = sr$, where s is the proportion saved from non-wage income. (Morishima[4] has shown how this is the special form of the general equation.) This agreeable simple form has led Robinson to argue that s and g (given by 'animal spirits') determine r. In a mathematical sense this is so since one has one equation and one unknown. But it would be much safer to say that s and g allow us to find r which may be consistent with balanced growth at the rate g. Since we have the n neo-classical equations still, the interpretation we can put on r as far as the individual producer is concerned is the same as before. Moreover it is I fear simply wrong to claim that the general form $g = n(r,p)$ leads to indeterminacy while the special form does not.

I can now, after this detour, explain more clearly why I do not think that special, social class savings functions as such lead to an interesting modification of neo-classical distribution theory.[5] In the special case just discussed all that we attain is a convenient decomposition of (n + 1) equations of which one involves only one unknown. To find the share of wages we must solve for p, we must add all the outputs and value them at p and we must add up all the labour demanded. No simple distribution theory emerges and in particular it is in no essentials different from the neo-classical one. It is only when the special savings assumptions are combined with a radically different view of what producers do and of the constraints under which they do it, as is for instance done by Kaldor, that a real dent in the neo-classical picture emerges. In this book I did not take such radical steps. Consequently I used the sociological savings hypothesis to discuss disequilibria and short period equilibria rather than steady states. For it was only then that these special assumptions were likely to lead to interesting new results.

In this I seem to differ from others who use the same approach. Robinson finds in the special savings assumption the theory of the steady state rate of profit. I was somewhat contemptuous of steady states and certainly not interested in them. In any case my concern was with shares. Kaldor in his earliest formulation[6] closed his system by postulating full employment. I was not prepared to do this and in consequence used a rather crude theory of entrepreneurial behaviour under uncertainty (chapter 3) to complete the system. My procedure here has a family resemblance to that of Robinson when she makes the rate of accumulation depend on the rate of profit.[7] But my essential objection to the neo-classical construction was not on grounds of logic but on realism and relevance. In particular the Keynesian influence is very strong and led me to regard full employment steady states with disfavour. I criticise the use of the elasticity of substitution (chapter 1) for instance, not so much on grounds of aggregation difficulties (although they are noted) as on the grounds that authors had wrongly taken labour as determining its real wage and had used quantity equations procedures. The second influence was that of Kalecki and the Robinson of Imperfect Competition days. Once again the objection to the neo-classical construct was not on the grounds that it was logically defective but that it was empirically ill-founded. Indeed in a theory in which variations in profit margins play a central rôle, perfect competition would have been an uncomfortable assumption. But throughout it was my view that full equilibria require the description of conditions in which all agents were satisfied, that these conditions were complex and numerous and that they would not yield a simple distribution theory. On the other hand I thought that in the study of disequilibria the broad direction of the movement of distributive shares could be deduced from rather general considerations which included the special savings function. I took the world to be typically out of full equilibrium.

The question of simplicity brings me back to the present. Since the rigorous neo-classical theory is far too complex to allow one even satisfactory taxonomic propositions of the kind that in the steady state the share of wages will be higher than it is in another if such and such is true, it is not unnatural that people have looked for drastic short cuts. In particular it has often been the case that a neo-classical theory has been attempted in terms of aggregate production functions and aggregates like capital.[8] Except under absurdly unrealistic assumptions such an aggregate theory cannot be shown to follow from the proper theory and in general is therefore open to severe logical objections. For instance it is not in general possible to argue that the steady state with a lower interest rate must on some index of capital always have more capital per man that the steady state with a higher interest rate.

It is extremely unfortunate, and to some extent the fault of its practitioners, that neo-classical theory has come to be identified with this aggregation version. On purely theoretical grounds there is nothing to be said in its favour. The view that nonetheless it 'may work in practice' sounds a little bogus and in any case the onus of proof is on those who maintain this. I am glad to see that I did not believe this argument in 1951 and sorry to see that I nonetheless every so often slipped into the aggregate version of the neo-classical model.

I sum up. In the last twenty years there has appeared a rigorous, logically coherent and beautiful version of the neo-classical economy in equilibrium. This description has no causal significance but describes states which are consistent with what we have defined as equilibrium. In this world the private marginal productivity interpretation of prices and interest rates is possible. The theory yields no propositions in terms of a few parameters in the theory of relative shares of the two main groups: wage earners and others. A sociological savings theory does not alter this fact. When the aggregated version of the theory is used simplicity is obtained at the cost of logical coherence, and in general such theories give the wrong answers in the sense that one can construct examples from the proper theory which make any one such answer wrong.

As far as this book is concerned, I recognised the absence of simple propositions. It was, and is, my view that a similar lack will be found in any proper equilibrium theory of a decentralised economy. However I did not take the neo-classical full equilibrium as being a description of any actual state. In particular I disliked the full employment postulate and the absence of a description of the investment process. (Investment, in neo-classical theory of the full employment type, is what it is because equilibrium requires it to be what it is.) I disliked the postulate of perfect competition. I thought that it might be possible by the aid of the special savings postulate to analyse the direction in which distributive shares moved in disequilibrium without necessarily being able to compare equilibrium shares. As a result most of what I have to say concerns disequilibria and I believe this to be the right approach.

II

I can now attempt to make clearer what this book is about and also note some of its most notable shortcomings.

My purpose was to provide a theory of relative shares of which the orthodox theory was a special case applicable in long run equilibrium only. While the orthodox theory in question was modified to allow for imperfect competition I conceived it as essentially neo-classical. I was not therefore concerned to topple this theory but allowed it full scope in the sphere for which it is designed – the regular progressing economy. In the analysis of other states I thought the theory to be of relatively little use. I thought that a classical wage fund approach was much more satisfactory to analyse actual situations where the goods available are the outcome of past decisions made under conditions of imperfect foresight. I believed that for such situations the special savings hypothesis provided a useable short cut to a macro-economic theory of shares. I noted in particular that in analysing actual movements, the share of wages might often move in a direction opposite to the (notional) equilibrium share. In particular I did not think that in the description of actual processes the equilibrium theory was of paramount importance. A typical argument for instance is on page 149:

> 'In a rapidly expanding capitalist economy, as Marx I think rightly conceived, the share of wages is kept low because of the high proportion of income which, on the average, is invested. It matters little in this connection that Marx, in common with other classical economists, held a fallacious theory of value.'

While I now have reservations on the question whether the basic savings assumption is correct (I state it as if it were universally agreed!) and doubt that in spite of my attempt in chapter 4 to be less aggregative, that so simple a theory can suffice, I am still in complete agreement with the basic position which I adopted.

The main shortcomings are lack of rigour at some crucial points, slipping into aggregation error and too simple a view of adjustment processes.

The questions I wished to study give rise to complicated non-linear time dependent equations which I could not solve. The result is that in a number of places I rely on a verbal exposition of essentially mathematical problems and some of the claims may be false or incompletely analysed.

Although, I believe, I understood the aggregation difficulty, there is too much in the book which relies on the 'representative firm' and occasionally on aggregate production functions. I now believe this to be a vital flaw. It may well be that it is an illusion to hold the view that there are any macro-economic shortcuts.

In my study of disequilibria I took Marshall as having established once and for all that money wages lag behind prices (page 101). This, in 1971, is an unhappy view to have taken. More than that, it may seriously upset the study of disequilibrium adjustment set forth in this book, when the post-ulate is dropped. It will certainly complicate it.

There are of course many other things I would now wish to treat quite differently. The crude uncertainty theory is one of these. But although I am aware of these many faults I believe that there are some virtues. The reader must judge. I have only made these changes in the text; I have deleted one erroneous section from the chapter on the history of the analysis of innovations (chapter 10) and changed two footnotes in chapter 3. I am grateful to J. McIntosh for preparing the Index.

F.H. Hahn

Introduction

I

The theory of distribution currently held by most economists is directly derived from the assumption that entrepreneurs maximise their money profits. This assumption implies 1) that in equilibrium the marginal cost of any one factor will be equal to its marginal revenue product and 2) that for any level of output the ratio of the marginal products of the factors will equal the ratio of their marginal costs. These two equilibrium conditions, given the supply conditions of the factors, the demand and production functions, are sufficient to determine the distribution of the revenue of any one firm among the factors used by it. On the basis of this analysis the distribution of income for the whole system can then be determined. Given the consumers' preference function, the supply conditions of the factors and the various production functions, we can uniquely determine the equilibrium distribution of factor income, i.e. that distribution of income at which any firm has maximised its money profits subject to the condition that all other firms have also maximised their profits.

The above is an outline of the framework of modern distribution theory. From it can be derived all recent contributions to the discussion such as Hicks' elasticity of substitution propositions and Kalecki's theory based on the degree of monopoly. Also since second order conditions of stable equilibrium are easily calculable, the effect of a change in any one of the parameters of the system on the distribution of income can be determined. The theory may appear complete.

Yet it is not as complete as might appear at first sight. Even at a purely formal level certain difficulties arise. These are mainly concerned with the equilibrium level of profits. As long as we adhere to a static analysis and the assumption of perfect competition this particular difficulty does not arise, since profits would be zero.[1] But once the assumption of perfect competition is dropped, as it must be, profits will have some positive value. The present theory however only helps us in determining relative profits in equilibrium,[2] namely as that structure of profits at which no one can increase his own profits by moving from one industry to another. To determine the level of profits, we must postulate a supply function of entrepreneurs. At present, this matter is left completely vague.

Thus it is said that each industry will be in equilibrium when profits are normal, and profits are normal when the industry is in equilibrium.[3] Clearly this will not do. To make the equilibrium determinate we must therefore have a supply function of entrepreneurs, existing ones and potential ones, to each industry. This could be done by assuming all entrepreneurs to be homogeneous, i.e. of equal ability, quality, etc., and to assume their supply to be perfectly elastic at a (marginal) profit equal to their (marginal) earnings in non-entrepreneurial occupations.[4] But such an assumption, while making our system determinate, would be highly unrealistic. On the other hand it would be in accordance with the main assumption of the theory, that everyone is out to maximise their money gain. It would also be in accordance with the static assumptions of the theory.

But although the theory would now be complete, its level of abstraction would be extremely high and in fact it could not hope to explain the actual distribution of income at any one moment of time (although it would be a useful first approach).

But what if we slightly relax the static assumptions and allow our model to explain the short run equilibrium distribution of income? The trouble now would be that the assumption that entrepreneurs maximise their money profits would not even be precise. Does it mean, for instance, as far as entrepreneurs are concerned, that the entrepreneurs maximise their money profit for a given moment of time without regard to future profits or do they maximise an expected stream of profit? The outline of the theory given above clearly assumes the former, while no doubt most economists agree that the maximisation of an expected stream of profits is the more reasonable of the two hypotheses. It can be argued that the theory could easily be modified to take account of this change in assumptions. This is no doubt so, and it has been done.[5]

But once we take the maximisation of a stream of expected profits as our basis for analysis, we must take account of entrepreneurs' expectations, and their attitude to risk. The subjective element thus becomes far more important than in the simpler static model and the question arises why we should persist in using the maximisation of money profits rather than of the entrepreneurs' utility.[6] Certainly nothing is gained in definiteness or precision by sticking to the money formula and there are some obvious gains in generality as well as conformity with the analysis of consumers' behaviour to be derived from the utility approach.

Many economists however have been reluctant to take this step, on the grounds that 1) the theory would become tautological and meaningless and 2) that we should forego the possibility of predicting entrepreneurial behaviour. It is true that the statement that 'a man will do what he prefers to do' is neither helpful nor meaningful. But the maximisation of utility assumption can yield fruitful results *provided* we can assume that entrepreneurial behaviour is consistent – or, to put it differently, that their utility functions do not change. If this assumption can be made then the conditions of maximum utility will yield us meaningful, i.e. testable propositions. For we shall be able to state the second order conditions and thus be able to predict the effect of certain changes in any one of the variables on entrepreneurial behaviour. Our prediction can them be tested against the entrepreneurs' actual reaction.

It is true that we have assumed the entrepreneurs' utility function to be given and constant. But of course our theory would be unaffected if the utility function were to be assumed to be changing in a given way. For practical purposes of prediction we would require concrete information not only of the form of the utility function but also of the way it is changing over time and in given circumstances. To make this information available would no doubt require sociologists and anthropologists as well as economists. But there is no inherent reason why it should be impossible to acquire this knowledge. Moreover this information would also be required if we continued to assume the maximisation of long run money profits, for we would have to determine the entrepreneurs' attitude to uncertainty and the way his expectations are formed. There is thus nothing gained by this procedure. In subsequent chapters we shall therefore use the assumption that entrepreneurs (potential and actual) maximise their utility rather than their long run money profits and explore some of the implications of this on the theory of distribution.

But the question may still be asked – why assume maximisation at all? The answer is of course that the assumption of maximisation of utility is only another way of assuming consistent behaviour on the part of the entrepreneur.[7] Unless we can assume such consistent behaviour or unless we know how it changes, any enquiry in the social sciences is doomed to failure. The very existence of the social sciences testifies to the common assumption that there is at least some consistency in human behaviour. The assumption that entrepreneurs maximise their utility is thus in no way different from the basic assumption on which the existence of the social sciences rests.

Of course the assumption that entrepreneurs maximise their utility will not by itself yield results significantly different from those of the maximum profit analysis unless further assumptions are introduced. In particular it is well known that the second order conditions of maximum utility yield ambiguous results, and in due course special assumptions will have to be made.[8] With the aid of these we shall first construct a simple short run equilibrium model of the share of wages.

In this simplified model the orthodox theory of distribution, relying as it does on the twin foundation of the production function and the elasticity of demand will appear as a special case. For in addition to these two determinants of the share of wages we shall make use of the relation which exists between the latter and the propensity to consume on the one hand and the willingness to supply output on the other. Since on the whole aggregate demand is an increasing and aggregate supply a diminishing function of the share of wages the equilibrium share of wages will be that share which equates the two.

II

But this simple model will abstract from all time lags and will be greatly dependent for its validity on the particular assumptions concerning the psychological propensities of producers. It will also only provide us with a short run theory of distribution. Most of the rest of this book will be devoted to exploring the consequences of dropping these assumptions.

The importance of lags to the theory of distribution can hardly be exaggerated. For on the one hand they rehabilitate a considerable part of classical writings on this topic and on the other throw grave doubts on the usefulness of equilibrium analysis.

Thus the fact that supply tends to lag behind demand, means that at any one moment of time the total amount of output available is completely determined by past decisions. The classical assumption of a given total output out of which more can be devoted to investment only at the expense of consumption regains much of its validity. In particular if demand exceeds supply there are only two ways in which this discrepancy can be met: 1) either stocks are decumulated or 2) prices rise. If now for any reasons there are periods of continuous excess demand only 2) will be practicable, and this will have considerable effect on the share of wages for it implies that producers are continuously on the inelastic part of their short run supply curves. Similarly periods of excess supply will have certain special effects on the share of wages.

Of course we cannot follow the classicals in speaking of fixed wage funds, nor can we follow them in their analysis of how money wages are determined. But on the other hand the fact remains that the output of wage goods in any one period is determined by past decisions and wage earners in any one period will not be able to consume more of these than are available (except by a decumulation of stocks). Hence if the ratio of wage goods to total output is diminishing for any reason whatsoever, then this will in practice imply that the share of wages in terms of wage goods will be diminishing, i.e. prices of wage goods will rise. Of course this will induce producers to supply more of these in the future. But if demand is increasing as fast or faster than wage goods can be supplied, their prices will not fall again but may even rise further. Much of what follows will be devoted to examining this and similar possibilities in greater detail.

But lags are also important in their effect on the ratio in which factors (labour and capital) are combined in production. The present theory assumes that an entrepreneur starts with zero commitments and then decides on that factor combination which will minimise his costs for any particular output. But this in the real world is in practice only possible for new producers who are only a small fraction of all producers. Normally producers will have entered into past commitments which restrict the degree to which they can adjust to a minimum cost factor combination, so that these past commitments will play an important part in determining the distribution of income in any one period.[9] Also it takes time before the supply of certain factors – especially capital equipment – can be increased. Thus there may be periods of considerable and continuous (relative) scarcity of capital and this will tend to lead to the substitution of the more readily available (and therefore cheaper) factor for the less readily available (and therefore more expensive) factor, and this again will have its effects on the distribution of income. It must be emphasised that it is once again the lags which are responsible for this relative scarcity of certain factors – their long run supply curve may be perfectly elastic. These and connected problems will be discussed in some detail in what follows.

The existence of lags also throws doubts on the usefulness of equilibrium analysis. This is not to say that the latter has not helped us considerably in getting our basic ideas straight, nor does it imply that lags make equilibrium impossible. But the existence of lags makes continued disequilibrium much more probable. Let us consider this in further detail.

If there were no investment at all then indeed lags or no lags, equilibrium of some sort would tend to be established sooner or later. But investment does take place continuously and this in itself may imply disequilibrium. For people invest not only because they expect demand to be increasing, but also because it has increased in the past and they found that they had insufficient capital – i.e. were not in long run equilibrium. Thus in many ways the existence of investment (or disinvestment) is an indication that long run equilibrium has not been achieved.

But recently the concept of an equilibrium rate of growth has gained ground[10] although no one has suggested that any known economy has ever attained it for any length of time. In a later chapter we shall examine the precise conditions for such a dynamic equilibrium to be achieved and shall show that these are so stringent and so dependent on a number of exogenous factors such as innovations and population growth, as to make its attainment altogether improbable on *a priori* grounds. Now if there were no lags this would not matter, for we could simply compare a series of equilibrium positions. But the existence of lags implies that except in the special case of an equilibrium rate of growth, there will always be disequilibrium somewhere in the economy.

The present day theory of distribution on the other hand is essentially a static equilibrium theory and for the reasons outlined seems therefore inadequate. But whether it has proved useful or not, almost all that can be said in the framework of its assumptions has been said, and apart from certain modifications already mentioned which we shall suggest, very little that is fruitful can be gained by further refinement. If economic theory is to make any progress it must be by a continuous widening of the field to which it can be applied; that is to say it must be based on as few unverified (or unverifiable) assumptions as possible. Clearly in this process we must lean heavily on the conclusions of simple models and everything in this essay must be regarded as an attempt to extend the present theory of distribution rather than to provide a new theory. We have accordingly concentrated on examining changes in the share of wages under certain conditions rather than on further refinement of equilibrium conditions. Complete equilibrium implies that everyone is as well off as he can make himself, in given circumstances. But we know that in a capitalist economy which has not stagnated such a position is never reached. There is therefore every justification for attempting to describe and analyse certain implications of disequilibrium.

Unfortunately in an attempt to 'dynamise' the theory of distribution we run into serious difficulties as far as the tools of analysis are concerned. The easiest of these to handle are linear difference (or differential) equations. But, unhappily, the number of cases in which we can use these is strictly limited.

For we shall frequently wish to examine cases where rising (or falling) incomes are accompanied by rising (or falling) prices. There is no way in which this can be done with difference equations without altering the coefficients. But once the coefficients are not constant, the difference equation will normally cease to be linear, and I know of no method by which such a non-linear difference equation can be solved.

But even when we abstract from price changes, we would be restricted to examining only those cases where everything is produced under constant returns at every moment of time. This, however, for reasons to be discussed is not a reasonable assumption when the rate of growth in income is changing and once again the difference equation breaks down. Moreover the impact of innovations and population changes must normally change the coefficients of our equations.

Being denied the use of different equations, our analysis will lose not only in elegance but in precision. Whatever may be thought of the applicability of mathematics to economics in general, there can be no doubt at all that in the case of dynamic analysis it is immensely useful, and reliance on purely literary discussion is fraught with dangers. In the circumstances however we have no alternative and we can do no more than hope that this handicap has not made our analysis altogether useless.

III

In this book the following basic definitions will be used:

1 The share of wages, unless otherwise specified, will refer to the share of net income (i.e. net of depreciation and decumulated stocks) going to wage earners.

2 By real wages we shali normally mean the wage of labour in terms of wage (consumption) goods. We shall however frequently make the assumption that relative prices and wages remain constant, so that any movement in real wages as defined above will coincide with movements in real wages when these are defined in terms of the own-product of labour.

3 The definition of a factor of production is fraught with difficulties and it has recently been suggested to avoid the term altogether and speak of specific inputs instead.[11] For our purposes however some sort of definition must be attempted. We accordingly define as labour the services of all those people whose income is conventionally, e.g. by tax authorities, described as wages. We also assume that, either the people making up that group are identical in all respects, or that the composition of the group remains the same throughout. By this definition and assumption we avoid the metaphysical speculations concerning the difference between 'factors' of production, and at the same time make possible a statistical verification of any results we may reach.

These are the basic definitions used. Others will be inserted as we go along and difficulties arising from them pointed out.

We also make the following basic assumptions: money wages and movements in money wages are exogenously determined. This does not mean that we shall be completely agnostic on this topic. For instance we shall expect money wages to vary with employment and the price level. What the assumption however does amount to is that we are not going to attempt to provide a theory of the determination of money wages. The assumption is made because we wish to avoid a detailed analysis of trade union bargaining, a topic on which *a priori* theorising seems particularly fruitless. We shall of course examine the effects of different and changing money wages on the share of wages, but will, by and large, take such changes as given.

IV

The book falls into two main parts. The first and shorter part will be devoted to a re-examination of two recent static theories of distribution and to an attempt to provide a short run theory of the share of wages which is based on the assumption that entrepreneurs maximise their utility and which is couched in the language of general rather than partial equilibrium analysis.

The second and longer part is devoted to the analysis of dynamic problems and therefore, by and large, of disequilibrium. After a preliminary survey of some of the problems involved we shall consider in detail the share of wages in the trade cycle, the effects of innovations on the share of wages, and lastly other long run influences on the share of wages will be examined.

Lastly we must stress that this book is concerned with the theory of distribution, and it has been found impossible to do more than give occasional references to the statistics of the problem. A number of data have been consulted and have been found not inconsistent with our results. But to present and analyse these in any detail would require a thesis on its own. It has often been said that statistics can be used to prove anything, and while this is certainly an exaggeration, it is probably true of sketchy and incompletely analysed data. Rather than use these, we have mostly avoided them altogether.

Chapter 1

The production function approach to the theory of distribution

I

Until relatively recently, most theories of distribution, as indeed most theories of value, were based on the assumption of perfect competition. In consequence, since it could easily be shown that except in the case of external economies (or increasing returns) to the industry, all factors of production including the entrepreneur would receive a reward equal to their marginal product and that the sum of these rewards would exhaust the total product of the industry (firm), the distribution of income between the factors was uniquely determined by their relative prices and the form of the production function. Thus if

$$X = F(a,b,c, \text{etc.}), \quad (1.1)$$

(where X is output and a, b, and c are quantities of factors A, B and C) is a production function such that

$$\lambda X = F(\lambda a, \lambda b, \lambda c, \text{etc.}), \quad (1.2)$$

(where λ is any arbitrary constant), then by Euler's theorem

$$X = F_a a + F_b b + F_c c + \text{etc.}, \quad (1.3)$$

(where subscripts denote differentiation). So that if the prices (w^a, w^b, etc.) of (n – 1) factors are given and entrepreneurs maximise their profit, i.e. the wage of any variable factor is equal to its marginal product, then the nth factor must also receive a reward equal to its marginal product.

If we let π be the price of the product then the condition of equilibrium in a perfectly competitive industry requires that

$$\pi X = \pi(F_a a + F_b b + F_c c \text{ etc.})$$
$$= w^a a + w^b b + w^c c \text{ etc.} \quad (1.4)$$

From this model the relative shares of any two factors can easily be calculated. If we let W^a, W^b, etc. be the real total income of factors A, B, etc. respectively then

$$\frac{W^a}{W^b} = \frac{aF_a}{bF_b}; \; \frac{W^a}{W^c} = \frac{aF_a}{cF_c}, \quad (1.5)$$

and since in equilibrium, minimum cost requires that

$$\frac{w^a}{w^b} = \frac{F_a}{F_b}; \; \frac{w^a}{w^c} = \frac{F_a}{F_c} \text{ etc.}, \quad (1.6)$$

and since F_a, F_b etc. are uniquely defined by the production function, knowledge of the latter and of relative factor prices was sufficient to determine the distribution of income.

If then we are given the supply function of the various factors of production, their demand can be derived from the production functions and consumer demand functions, and the equilibrium distribution of income can be uniquely determined not only for any particular industry but for the economy as a whole.

This model of distribution has a number of drawbacks which can be classified under two main headings.

1 The model is based on too highly simplified assumptions concerning the nature of competition. Not much need be said about this here. Most economists I think would agree today that perfect competition can be regarded as no more than a very first approximation to the happenings of the real world, nor will it be seriously disputed that the motivations ascribed to the units of decision, in particular the maximisation of money profits, are far too mechanical and simple. In the following two chapters we shall have occasion to examine various attempts to build a more realistic theory, and we postpone further consideration of these problems until then.

2 The model, in common with a large number of similar ones, is entirely static. Now as was pointed out in the introduction there is nothing reprehensible in static analysis as such, provided we can be sure that the static stability conditions which can be derived from the model will be in fact

satisfied. To show this, as Samuelson has pointed out,[1] requires a dynamic theory, and most of the theories of distribution available have not provided such a theory. This problem of providing a dynamic theory falls into two main parts:

a *Partial Analysis.*
When dealing with the individual firm or industry, then as will be shown presently, we are mostly in a position to make realistic assumptions which will ensure dynamic stability and thus enable us to formulate comparative statics propositions. After all, few economists would suggest than an explosive cobweb for instance is a typical adjustment path of a significant part of a country's industry.

b *General Equilibrium Analysis.*
Here the problem is far more complicated. A great majority of economists for instance consider the trade cycle as one of the typical phenomena of a capitalist society. If they are in fact correct then equilibrium will be the exception rather than the rule and it is difficult to see how a comparative statics analysis can be successfully applied.

We shall now consider both these problems in some detail in so far as they affect the distribution of income theory derived from the perfect competition model.

II

We shall first consider an individual industry in isolation. From the above model, assuming that the supply of factors to the industry is perfectly elastic we can derive the following second order conditions:

1 for each firm marginal costs must be increasing in equilibrium and
2 for each firm the marginal rate of substitution between factors must be increasing (the production contours must be convex to the origin).

From these second order conditions it is possible to derive a number of interesting results, provided instantaneous adjustment is assumed. Thus for instance it is possible to predict that a fall in the wage of any factor, all other things being equal, must increase the amount of that factor employed. For 2) above ensures that the consequent substitution effect will always be favourable to the factor the price of which has fallen. Since we have assumed linear and homogeneous production functions the expansion effect must also be favourable to our factor.

We have already seen that in the above model the distribution of income in the industry is uniquely determined by the relative prices of the factors and the form of the production function. A change in either of these will therefore tend to affect the equilibrium distribution of income. Changes in the form of the production function and their effect on distribution are examined in a later chapter. Here we shall concentrate our attention on the effects of changes in relative factor prices.

If we assume that there are only two factors of production A and B and that w^b remains constant when w^a falls, then we know from our second order conditions that the amount of A employed must increase. If we then differentiate (1.5) with respect to a, we can easily find the conditions which must be fulfilled in order that a fall in w^a should lead to an increase in A's share in the income of the industry. These conditions are best summarised by a measure called the elasticity of substitution.[2] (σ)

There are three main definitions of the elasticity of substitution:

1 Hicks'[3] definition which gives $\sigma = \dfrac{F_a F_b}{xF_{ab}}$

2 Robinson's[4] definition which gives $\sigma = \dfrac{E\left(\frac{a}{b}\right)}{E\left(\frac{F_a}{F_b}\right)}$ where E is a Champernowne notation for d Log ( ) and

3 Champernowne's[5] definition which gives $\sigma = \dfrac{E(x)}{EF_b}$ (b constant).

These three definitions can be shown to be identical under conditions of constant returns to scale.[6] Robinson's and Hicks' definitions refer to one given isoquant. Champernowne's definition is not thus restricted and is therefore independent of the conditions of returns.

It is clear that if the elasticity of substitution is to be useful, the prices of factors must either be equal to or proportional to their marginal products. From which it follows that Robinson's and Hicks' definitions give rise to difficulties if the production function is not both linear and homogeneous. For if the production functions are not of this type, then some factors at least must receive a reward in excess of, or less than, and not necessarily proportional to their marginal products. But even if this residual is proportional to the marginal product of a factor receiving it we cannot assume this proportion to remain constant. This does not mean that Hicks' or Robinson's formulae could not be adapted to deal with this problem. Such adaptation however is not easily made, since one would have to know the degree of economies (or diseconomies) of scale associated with the increase of any given factor.

If however there are constant returns to scale, and the price of B remains constant when w^a changes, then knowledge of the elasticity of substitution is sufficient to determine the effect of the change in w^a on the distribution of factor incomes. If $\sigma > 1$ when w^a falls, then the proportionate fall in the ratio of the marginal product of A to the marginal product of B will be less than the proportionate increase in the ratio of A to B employed, and hence A's relative share will increase. The reverse is the case when $\sigma < 1$ when w^a falls. We shall call these the 'normal' conditions for an increase or decrease in A's relative share when w^a falls.

But we have assumed w^b constant throughout. But a change in w^a may affect the demand for B and whether or not w^b then remains constant will depend on the conditions under which B is supplied. It can be easily shown that the 'cross-elasticity' of demand $\frac{\partial b}{\partial w^a}\frac{w^a}{b}$ (call it ϵ) for B and when w^a falls is given by the simple equation[7]

$$\epsilon = \frac{W^a}{X}\,(e - \sigma)$$

Whenever $\epsilon = 0$, the demand for B will change when w^a changes and hence the supply conditions of B must be taken into account before we can determine whether $\frac{w^a}{w^b}$ will change in the same direction as w^a has changed. Three main cases have been distinguished.[8]

1 If the elasticity of supply of B $(\eta = \frac{\partial w^b}{\partial b}\ \frac{b}{w^b}) > 0$ then

a) if $\epsilon < 0$ $(e > \sigma)$, a fall in w^a must increase w^b and a rise in w^a diminish w^b. Δw^a and $\Delta\left(\frac{w^a}{w^b}\right)$ must be of the same sign.

b) if $\epsilon > 0$ $(e < \sigma)$ then a fall in w^a will lead to a fall in w^b and a rise in w^a to a rise in w^b. But if the fall in w^a and therefore in costs either leaves the output of the firm constant or increases it, then a diminution in B must mean that the marginal product of B has risen relatively to that of A, i.e. that $\left(\frac{w^a}{w^b}\right)$ has diminished. Similarly if a rise in w^a either leaves output constant or diminishes it, then an increase in B must mean a diminution in its marginal product and a rise in that of A, i.e. $\frac{w^a}{w^b}$ must increase.

But Kahn is surely wrong when he considers this argument conclusive proof of the assertion that $\Delta\left(\frac{w^a}{w^b}\right)$ must always be of the same sign as Δw^a whenever $\eta > 0$ irrespective of whether $\epsilon > 0$ or < 0. For he is assuming that a given increase in A will always be absorbed. But what for instance of the case where the demand curve for the product is backward rising? In that case there is no reason to assume that the increase in A will be absorbed and it is perfectly possible for a reduction in w^a to lead to an increase in $\left(\frac{w^a}{w^b}\right)$, and a reduction in the output of the firm.

But we may wish to rule out the case of a backward rising demand curve for the product since this would be incompatible with stable perfect competition equilibrium. If we do so then our proposition must be as follows: if the price of B falls in the same proportion as w^a has fallen, and the demand curve for the final product is not backward rising, then the demand for B will either remain the same or be greater than it was before the fall in w^a. It therefore follows that the demand curve for B will be shifted to the left (because $\epsilon > 0$) in such a manner that for a price of B equal to w^b_1 when $\frac{w^b - w^b_1}{w^b} = \frac{\Delta w^a}{w^a}$, the demand for B will be the same or greater than it was when the price of B was w^b and w^a had not fallen. Therefore the intersection of the new demand curve for B with B's supply curve will be at a point where the price of $B > w^b_1$ and therefore $\frac{w^a}{w^b}$ will fall when w^a falls.

Thus if we can exclude a backward rising demand curve for the product, $\Delta\left(\frac{w^a}{w^b}\right)$ will always be of the same sign as Δw^a, and the share of A will increase when $\Delta w^a < 0$ when $\sigma > 1$ and when $\Delta w^a > 0$, when $\sigma < 1$.

2 If the supply curve of B is forward falling $\eta < 0$ then:

a) if $\epsilon < 0$ a fall in w^a will lead to a fall in w^b and a rise in w^a to a rise in w^b. It is therefore clear that $\Delta\left(\frac{w^a}{w^b}\right)$ may not be of the same sign as Δw^a. Now ϵ is the cross elasticity of demand for B when w^b is constant. Since $\epsilon < 0$, a fall in w^a will increase the demand for B at its old price, i.e. the demand curve for B is shifted to the right. If we now assume w^a constant at its new level, the new demand curve for B must be downward sloping. If now $\eta = \epsilon$ then when the demand for B increases when w^a falls but w^b constant, the supply price of B will fall in the same proportion as w^a has fallen. But the intersection of the new demand curve for B with the latter's supply curve will be to the right of the quantity of B demanded when w^b is constant. Therefore w^b will fall in more than proportion to w^a and $\Delta\left(\frac{w^a}{w^b}\right) > 0$ when $\Delta w^a < 0$. A diagram may make this clearer.

In figure 1 SS is the supply curve of B. $D_0 D_0$ and $D_1 D_1$ are the demand curves for B before and after the fall in w^a, assuming that w^a remains constant at its given value. PZ is the increase in demand for B when w^b is constant and w^a falls by a given amount. If now $\eta = \epsilon$ then $\frac{\Delta w^a}{w^a} = \frac{\Delta w^b}{w^b} = \frac{ZR}{ZN}$.[9] But equilibrium is attained at Q which is below R and therefore $\frac{\Delta w^b}{w^b} > \frac{\Delta w^a}{w^a} \left(\frac{\Delta w^b}{w^b} < 0,\ \frac{\Delta w^a}{w^a} < 0\right)$. Therefore if $\Delta\left(\frac{w^a}{w^b}\right)$

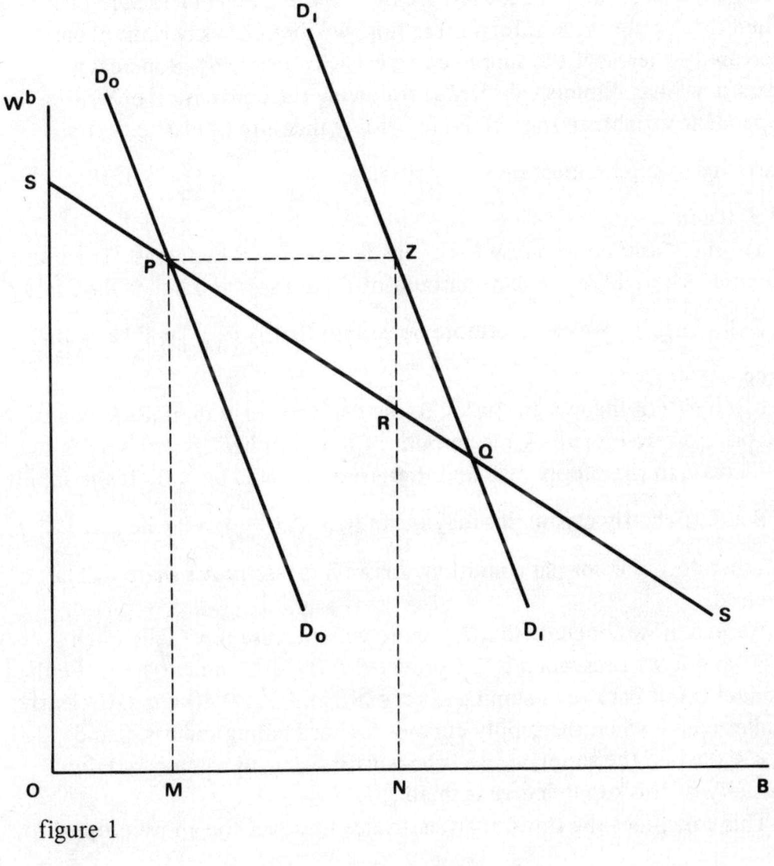

figure 1

is to be of the same sign as w^a the elasticity of supply of B must be less than the cross elasticity of demand for B. Unless this condition is fulfilled, the conditions for an increase in A's share when w^a changes are the reverse of the normal ones.

b) if $\epsilon > 0$ then when $\Delta w^a < 0$, Δw^b will be > 0 and when $\Delta w^a > 0$, Δw^b will be < 0. Therefore we can be certain that $\Delta \left(\frac{w^a}{w^b}\right)$ will be of the same sign as Δw^a, and the normal conditions for an increase in A's share will hold.

3 There remains the interesting case, first discussed in this context by Kahn, of a backward rising supply curve of B. Whereas a forward falling supply curve of B is given by the equation $w^b = f(B)$, a backward rising supply curve is written as $B = \phi(w^b)$, that is to say in the former case w^b is the dependent while in the latter case it is the independent variable. When the supply curve is forward falling, w^b diminishes because B has increased, whereas if the supply curve is backward rising, B increases because w^b has diminished. Hence following the convention of writing the dependent variable in the numerator of any measure of elasticity, the elasticity of supply must now be written as $\eta^* = \frac{\partial b}{\partial w^b} \frac{w^b}{b}$. If then $\eta^* < 0$ and

a) if $\epsilon < 0$ then when $\Delta w^a < 0$ the demand for B increases. Therefore the price offered for the same amount of B increases and hence the supply of B diminishes. We can therefore be certain that $\Delta \left(\frac{w^a}{w^b}\right)$ will be of the same sign as Δw^a.

b) if $\epsilon > 0$, then when $\Delta w^a < 0$, the demand for B diminishes, hence the price offered for the same amount of B diminishes. But this leads to an increase in the supply of B and therefore Δw^b will be < 0. If the supply of B is sufficiently elastic this may mean that $\Delta \left(\frac{w^a}{w^b}\right) > 0$ when $\Delta w^a < 0$ and therefore the normal conditions for an increase in A's share will be reversed.

We may now conclude that A's share will increase if w^a falls when $\sigma > 1$ and if w^a rises when $\sigma < 1$ provided i) the demand curve for the final product is not backward sloping when $\epsilon > 0$ and $\eta > 0$, ii) η is sufficiently smaller than ϵ when the supply curve is forward falling and $\epsilon < 0$ and iii) $\epsilon < 0$ when the supply curve is backward rising, or when $\epsilon > 0$ the elasticity of this supply curve is small.

This concludes the static analysis. Since however the above propositions are derived from static stability conditions we must now see whether these can in fact be used, that is whether dynamic stability conditions are satisfied also. This is especially important in this case, since it is generally recognised that it will take time for any given reorganisation in production to take place.

Let us consider the case of a forward falling supply curve of B first. We will assume that the demand for B is a function of its price in the previous period given w^a, but that the price of B reacts instantaneously to a change in the demand for it. It may be thought that these assumptions would lead to a cobweb type of adjustment once equilibrium is displaced. This however is not so. Our assumptions may be put in equation form as follows:

$$b_t = D(w^b_{t-1}), \quad (1.7)$$

$$w^b_t = S(b_t), \quad (1.8)$$

Solving this system for a small displacement in the neighbourhood of equilibrium we obtain

$$w^b_t = {}^o w^b + \left(\frac{S^o_b}{D^o_b}\right)^t \overline{w}^b, \quad (1.9)$$

where S^o_b and D^o_b are the slopes of the supply and demand curves referred to the price axis and ${}^o w^b$ is the equilibrium price of B and $\overline{w}^b$ is the given divergence from ${}^o w^b$. Dynamic stability then requires that $\left|\frac{S^o_b}{D^o_b}\right| < 1$.

But S_b and D_b are of the same sign, hence $\left(\frac{S^o_b}{D^o_b}\right) > 0$ and therefore we cannot have cobweb type oscillations. Moreover the static stability conditions are that $S_b < D_b$, hence in this case whenever we have static stability we also have dynamic stability.

Exactly the same applies to the case of a backward rising supply curve of B. Here our equations, making the same assumptions as before are

$$w^b_t = D(b_{t-1}), \quad (1.10)$$

$$b_t = S(w^b_t), \quad (1.11)$$

for which we obtain the solution

$$b_t = b^o + \bar{b}\left(\frac{D_b^o}{S_b^o}\right)^t \qquad (1.12)$$

where b^o is the equilibrium amount of B and $\bar{b}$ is the given divergence from b^o. Once again $\frac{D_b}{S_b} > 0$ and static stability requires $D_b < S_b$ so that dynamic and static stability conditions are the same.

The only case therefore where dynamic stability conditions may not be satisfied even though the static stability conditions are, arises when the supply curve of B is upward sloping. Static stability only requires that the supply curve should cut the demand curve from below; dynamic stability requires that in the neighbourhood of equilibrium the slope of the supply curve should be less than that of the demand curve when both these slopes refer to the quantity axis, and when supply lags behind price. If however as we are assuming demand lags behind price but supply does not, the reverse must be the case.

That means that if we can regard B as being produced under diminishing costs, dynamic stability conditions will always be satisfied when static stability conditions are satisfied. If however B is produced under steeply increasing costs then it is possible that dynamic instability may arise. In that case one particular firm will always find that its given combination of A and B is not the optimum or equilibrium combination and that its output is not the equilibrium output. The analysis of the elasticity of substitution which assumes that the firm is always in equilibrium will then not apply.

But unless we assume that dynamic stability conditions are not satisfied in the selling of the finished product, the above will be the only possibility of dynamic instability. In all other cases the comparative statics approach will yield the correct answer. Thus the elasticity of substitution as a tool for analysing changes in the distribution of the output of a firm or industry which occur when the price of one factor changes is extremely useful except in the case where the slope of the supply curve of B is steeper than that of the demand curve for B and $\epsilon \neq 0$. In that particular case this type of analysis will break down.

III

The question now arises of how far this sort of analysis can be applied usefully to the whole economy. Various difficulties become immediately apparent. Thus, what is the meaning that can be attached to the marginal product of a factor for the economy as a whole? This type of difficulty has been dealt with by a number of authors writing on what is now called the aggregation problem. They showed that provided we concern ourselves with very small displacements only and provided the production functions are of a certain form it is possible to devise a meaningful index of marginal productivity which will obey the same laws as does the marginal product of the factor in an individual sector. In what follows we shall assume that this particular problem has been adequately solved.

Another difficulty which arises is that when dealing with the whole economy, individual industries of which have not identical production functions, the commodity elasticity of substitution of consumers must be taken into account. Hicks has shown that this can be done by regarding the total elasticity of substitution as the algebraic sum of the technical and commodity elasticity of substitution.[10] While no doubt this is a valid formal solution it robs the concept of one of its chief attractions, namely that it could be regarded as a purely technical datum which could be derived from the objective and given production functions.

Lastly, as far as the static analysis is concerned, the difficulty arises of how to define the elasticity of demand for the output of the whole system. Two rival interpretations have been offered. Hicks, Robinson, Pigou and Kahn used the real elasticity of demand for all goods taken together and their prices expressed in terms of themselves. Since then the unit of measure of the composite output of the economy was a unit of that output itself, the elasticity of demand must always be infinitely high. Thus if this interpretation of the total elasticity of demand is used ϵ must always be < 0, since σ is always less than infinitely large.

Machlup on the other hand used a money elasticity of demand, which would always be equal to unity provided there is no net hoarding or dishoarding. Robinson, commenting on Machlup's use of this elasticity, held the view that 'for a discussion of the effect upon the share of labour in the real national income the demand for output must clearly be conceived in real terms'[11] and therefore rejected Machlup's use of the money elasticity of demand.

The question of which definition to use is clearly of some importance. It is doubtful whether any of the writers who used the real elasticity of demand would wish to do so today in the light of our present knowledge. For the use of the real elasticity of demand implies an acceptance of Say's Law, and of a classical homogeneous system of equations to represent the economy in which only relative money prices play any role, while the absolute level of money prices has no significance at all. Such a system is only legitimate if either the demand for money is identically equal to zero or independent of any of the variables in the system. Since however those are not assumptions which can legitimately be made, this type of system has in the main been abandoned by modern economists.

It is easily seen that Robinson's justification of using the real elasticity of demand is no justification at all. Whether to use the latter or not depends on whether the classical system is a legitimate one or not. It has nothing whatever to do with the fact that we are interested in labour's real and not in its money share. For if we know the money shares of all factors, this is expressed as a pure number and always equals its real share.

Machlup's use of the money elasticity of demand is to be preferred unless we believe the classical system to be adequate. But we must take care how we use it. Machlup's elasticity is clearly derived from the Quantity Equation. If V and M can be assumed constant then a given proportionate fall in prices must imply an equi-proportionate increase in output (since MV = PT). But we must make certain that the real volume of output is not already determined elsewhere in the system, say by the demand and supply of factors as functions of their real wage and the production functions. For in that case the money elasticity of demand could only tell us what change in the price level must follow an already given change in output and that, from our point of view, would be of no use. Quite apart from that we would again be dealing with a classical system. When we use the money elasticity of demand, we must therefore imply a system of equations, representing the economy, in which the money equation plays a part in determining the value of the real variables. Any Keynesian system will satisfy these conditions.

Now the elasticity of substitution theorists were always concerned with a comparison of stationary states in which net investment was zero and the propensity to consume unity. If we are concerned with thorough-going stationary states there will also be no uncertainty and hence no net hoarding. A fall in price may result in net dissaving since the real value of savings is increased. Once however the desired amount of savings is held, individuals will spend the whole of their income. It therefore follows that once the initial dissaving has taken place the money elasticity of demand for goods in general will be equal to unity, as Machlup assumed it to be. Therefore unless we accept the classical system and Say's Law in which the real level of output is independent of the absolute level of prices, which it clearly is not, we must use the money elasticity of demand and then clearly the transition from a partial to a general analysis does not enable us, as Kahn thought,[12] to exclude the possibility of $\epsilon > 0$.

But if the elasticity of substitution approach can only be applied to stationary states then clearly it will be of little use since the real world is not stationary. It is of course legitimate to analyse the stationary case as a first approximation, but we clearly cannot stop there if we wish to say something about the distribution of income in the real world. The question then is whether the approach outlined in this chapter can be extended to deal with a system in which there is positive net investment. Once net investment is introduced into our model it is difficult to keep the analysis static. In a later chapter this is attempted in a model of short period flow equilibrium, where all adjustments are assumed to be instantaneous. For our present purpose however, when we are concerned to assess the usefulness of the elasticity of substitution analysis it would be inappropriate to make too many restrictive assumptions. We must therefore face up to the dynamic problems involved.

At the outset we may hazard the opinion that the elasticity of substitution will not be a useful tool of analysis in the case where positive net investment is due to an income expansion from a depression to a boom. At a later stage we hope to show that in such a situation producers will on the average find that they have too little capital to produce at the optimum (minimum cost) factor ratio. Hence a fall in the price of any one factor, unless it is very substantial, may not lead to any substitution at all. This can be easily seen as follows. Assume that there are only two factors of production, labour and capital. Suppose further that in any one period the stock of capital available to any one firm is fixed, but that demand increases. Now assume a fall in money wages. The consequence is shown in figure 2 (on following page).

On the horizontal axis we measure units of labour, on the vertical axis units of capital. P_0P_0, P_1P_1 are isoquants. W_0W_0 is the budget line in period 0. At period 0 we assume the firm to produce an output P_0 at the optimum factor ratio (OM labour, OR capital). Suppose demand increases to P_1 but the stock of capital cannot be increased. Then at the higher output the firm will still be using OR of capital. If we assume constant returns to scale then to produce output P_1 at the optimum factor ratio would require OS units of capital. Hence the firm is not in long run equilibrium and relative factor prices are not equal to relative marginal products. If money

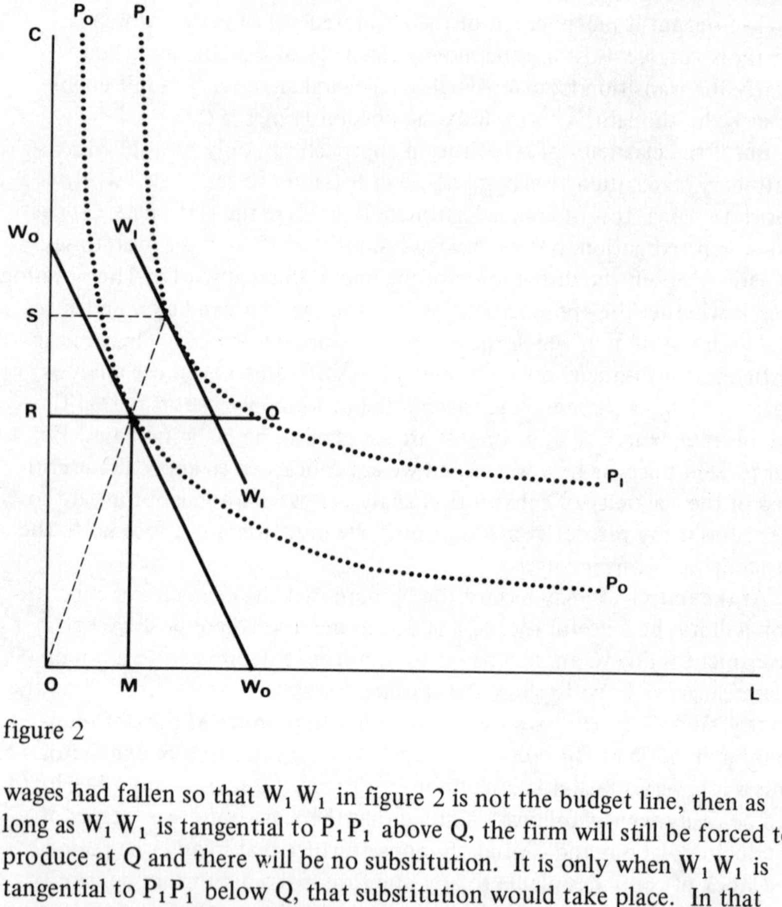

figure 2

wages had fallen so that $W_1 W_1$ in figure 2 is not the budget line, then as long as $W_1 W_1$ is tangential to $P_1 P_1$ above Q, the firm will still be forced to produce at Q and there will be no substitution. It is only when $W_1 W_1$ is tangential to $P_1 P_1$ below Q, that substitution would take place. In that case the demand for investment would fall sharply and the boom would probably come to an end.

We need of course not be surprised that the elasticity of substitution proves unhelpful whenever there is disequilibrium, for it is specifically designed to compare two equilibrium positions. In so far however as typical capitalist economies are subject to booms of the sort postulated, the distribution of income must remain unexplained as long as we rely exclusively on the production function approach to this problem. Exactly the same argument of course applies to the case of a depression with (undesired) excess capacity. Here the marginal cost of using capital is almost zero, and changes in the price of labour or capital will have no or a negligible substitution effect, quite apart from the fact that relative factor prices will not equal relative marginal products.

The only possibility remaining is that of a regular progressing economy, which we shall have occasion to discuss in some detail in a later chapter. Here we may note the following. The conditions of long run equilibrium with positive net investment are 1) that *ex ante* investment should equal *ex ante* savings and 2) that the rate of growth in output made possible by the rate of growth in the stock of capital and employment, should equal the rate of growth in demand. If we could assume instantaneous adjustments then the elasticity of substitution would remain a useful means of analysing the effect of a fall in the price of a factor upon its share. If this however can not be assumed then serious difficulties arise. For there is nothing in the nature of a regular progressing economy which ensures dynamic stability. Thus for instance a fall in wages leading to a fall in investment demand may give rise to continued oscillations or divergences from the equilibrium path. In other words it may be impossible to compare two equilibrium paths for the simple reason that the transition from one equilibrium to another is never accomplished. Hence the elasticity of substitution will only prove useful in analysing this case when we can be sure that dynamic stability conditions are satisfied.

IV

We are now in a position to appraise the 'production function' approach to the theory of distribution.

In appraising any theory we must ask two preliminary questions: 1) is it meaningful in the sense that it could conceivably be refuted by an appeal to facts and 2) is it useful in the sense that known facts do not contradict it?

The only way in which the meaningfulness and usefulness of a theory can be assessed is by an analysis of displacement from equilibrium. For as Samuelson has pointed out:

> 'It is hardly enough . . . to show that under certain conditions we can name enough relations (equations) to determine the values of our unknowns. It is important that our analysis be developed in such terms that we are aided in determining how our variables change qualitatively or quantitatively with changes in explicit data . . . In fact our theory is meaningless in the operational sense unless it does imply some restrictions

upon empirically observable quantities by which it could conceivably be refuted.'[13]

It is for these reasons that we have spent the greater part of this chapter in an analysis of displacements from equilibrium.

There can be little doubt that on this definition the theory under consideration is meaningful. The elasticity of substitution, the elasticity of supply of factors, and the elasticity of demand could all be ascertained empirically and therefore predictions could be made which would either be refuted or confirmed by events. No one however has ever attempted to make such predictions and it is therefore not easy to say whether the theory is useful or not.

But there are certain indirect ways in which the usefulness of the theory could be tested. For instance we know that the production function approach to distribution assumes that the economy is typically in equilibrium in the sense that each individual unit of decision is in its most preferred position. But we also know that capitalist economies are subject to more or less serious and continuous fluctuations, so that the assumption of continuous equilibrium is unlikely to be confirmed by the facts, and the theory is likely to apply to certain very special situations only. Again the greater part of the theory was developed on the assumption of stationary states with zero net investment and savings. This assumption will certainly not be fulfilled in the real world. Nor is the assumption of perfect competition and/or constant net profit margins likely to be confirmed by the facts.

There are thus a number of indications that the theory is too simple and abstract to be a sufficient guide for prediction and the interpretation of known facts. This as we have seen is particularly true when the theory is used to analyse, not the distribution of a firm's income between the factors it employs, but the distribution of the national income between factors of production. This however does not mean that the theory here discussed has not been useful as a first approach. The production function approach to the problem of distribution was a major intellectual achievement of modern economics, and any development of the theory of distribution will have to take account of it. For even if equilibrium is the exception rather than the rule, we need an equilibrium theory before we can hope to make any attempt to analyse disequilibria and to construct a dynamic theory.

So much for the general methodological difficulties encountered. We must now also note some of the special and more technical problems we have had to deal with.

1 We found that the partial analysis was incomplete in so far as it neglected to impose sufficient constraints to ensure that the comparison of two equilibrium positions was legitimate. This is the problem of dynamic stability conditions. We discovered that, paradoxically, the two exceptional cases of forward falling, or backward rising supply curves of a factor, were those in which static and dynamic stability conditions coincided and therefore the analysis was most complete, while in the more normal case of a rising supply curve of a factor additional constraints on the slopes of the relevant curves had to be imposed.

2 In the transition from partial to general analysis certain special difficulties were encountered. A choice had to be made between a classical system in which money is 'neutral' and a system in which it is not. We rejected the classical approach on the grounds that it conflicted with what we now know about the role of money in the system. This meant that we abandoned the real in favour of the money elasticity of demand for output as a whole, with certain consequences to what we have called the 'normal' conditions for an increase in a factor's share when its price changes.

We also noted that if we removed the restrictive stationary state assumptions, this led to the difficulty that dynamic general equilibrium may be unstable. We pointed out that much of modern trade cycle theory is based on the assumption that such an equilibrium is in fact unstable, so that if these theories are correct, a 'comparative dynamic equilibrium' approach to distribution may be impossible.

3 Lastly there remain the special problems which are encountered when the assumption of perfect competition is dropped. Some theorists have agreed that if this is done, the production function approach is useless and that other means must be found to analyse the distribution of income. It is time that these theories were examined.

Chapter 2
M. Kalecki's theory of distribution

In the previous chapter we have considered a theory of distribution which was mainly based on the production function. In this chapter we shall consider a theory which is mainly based on the demand curve, and which was first presented by Kalecki in a series of well known essays.[1] A discussion of Kalecki's views is important, both because his theory is important in its own right and because it focuses attention on an aspect of distribution theory which had hitherto been neglected because of the preoccupation of earlier writers with the production function and perfect competition.

I

Kalecki's position may be summarised as follows. Given an industry (defined by positive cross-elasticities of demand for the products of the various firms constituting it) and given a close similarity between the cost conditions of the various firms, together with the condition of constant average prime cost, we may write the ratio of gross profit per unit of output of the industry to the price per unit of output as $\frac{P_k - a_k}{P_k}$ (P_k equals price, a_k equals average prime cost), and identify this with the degree of imperfection of the market in which the industry sells its goods. (Since a_k equals marginal prime cost and since the latter is equated to marginal revenue, this may also be written as $\frac{1}{e}$ where e is the elasticity of demand.)

If now there is a fall in a_k, then it follows that $\frac{P_k - a_k}{P_k}$ has increased and there will therefore be an inducement to reduce price for:

> 'A cut of the price P_k by a certain percentage means a smaller percentage ~~means a smaller percentage~~ cut of $P_k - a_k$ than in the initial position. Consequently, if firms stick to their view of what are the expected percentage increases in their sales caused by a percentage cut in prices,

they must consider it profitable to reduce them. Now as long as $\frac{P_k - a_k}{P_k}$ remains greater than in the initial position the price fall goes on.'[2]

This process however may not take place if the degree of imperfection is increased or decreased by the fall in price.

Any change in the degree of imperfection will be represented by a change in $\frac{P_k - a_k}{P_k}$ except in the following cases.

1 Because the average costs of firms constituting the industry have not all fallen in the same proportion, so that any one producer changing P_k in response to a change in a_k, will also change the ratio of P_k to all the other prices and thus 'affect the position with regard to the expected reaction of sales in response to a change in price'.[3] This factor however is likely to be of little importance.

2 Because a bottleneck, where marginal and average prime cost sharply diverge, has been reached.

3 Because a change in the ratio of prime selling costs may be reflected in $\frac{P_k - a_k}{P_k}$.

If these factors are non-existent or very small, then the following conclusions are reached:

$$\text{Let} \quad \mu = \frac{\Sigma Q_k(P_k - a_k)}{\Sigma Q_k P_k}$$

which is the weighted average of profit margins and may in accordance with what has been said previously, be called the average degree of imperfection of the whole system. Let W equal the total wage bill, and mW the raw material bill. Total prime costs are then given by $(1 + m)W$. Also $1 - \mu$ must by definition be the proportion of total output going to prime costs, so that $\frac{\mu}{1 - \mu}$ is the ratio of gross profits to prime costs and,

$$\frac{\mu}{1 - \mu} \; (1 + m)W$$

equals gross profit. Now the net output is equal to the sum of gross profit and the wage bill and can be represented by $\frac{\mu}{1-\mu}(1+m)W+W$.

Therefore the relative share of wages, w, in the net output is given by

$$w = \frac{W}{\frac{\mu}{1-\mu}(1+m)W+W} = \frac{1-\mu}{1-\mu m}$$

Thus it is seen that w is a diminishing function of both μ and m, the degree of imperfection and the proportion of total wages spent on raw materials.

It remains to give Kalecki's justification of using 'purely short period considerations' to determine the distribution of the National Income at any one moment of time.

In his 'Distribution of the National Income' where Kalecki explicitly deals with this topic, he says that according to his formula 'the distribution of the National Income is at every moment determined by the degree of monopoly' and that therefore his formula 'holds both for the short period and the long run even though it was deduced on the basis of so to speak pure short period considerations.' This statement he substantiates as follows. Under imperfect competition 'long run equilibrium is represented by the normal use of such a type of equipment that with a given degree of monopoly, it is impossible to earn profits higher than normal by employing a different type'. Thus even if the basic data alter, and thus alter the long run equilibrium price, since 'its relation to the average cost of manual labour and raw material' does not alter 'because for all types of equipment the marginal cost curve coincides with the average cost curve of manual labour and raw materials and the degree of monopoly is supposed to be given', the distribution of the National Income continues to correspond to the short run formula. This is regarded as always true, as long as full capacity is not reached.

II

Kalecki's theory hinges on three basic assumptions: 1) that there is continuous excess capacity, 2) that marginal 'overhead' costs are small enough to be ignored and 3) that the concept of an average degree of monopoly is meaningful. All of these assumptions merit closer examination.

1 Kalecki is mainly concerned with that type of excess capacity which is both deliberate and permanent. This he ascribes to 'the large scale economies [which] prevent firms from reducing their plant below a certain

limit'. This type of excess capacity is presumably due to large indivisibilities in equipment. Whether it is reasonable to assume that the typical firm's equipment is of this type is a question of empirical fact. It may be worthwhile however to quote a recent view that many 'fixed factors' in manufacturing which were supposed as indivisible are in fact probably highly divisible.[4] A constant prime cost curve in strict theory is more compatible with a high degree of divisibility of equipment than with a low degree, so that the observed phenomenon of constant prime costs may be explained at least as well by a high divisibility in equipment as by a large excess capacity due to low divisibility.

The trouble however is that if we assume equipment – at least after a certain minimum like factory buildings etc. have been acquired – to be highly divisible we can no longer assume the entrepreneur to base all his price and output decisions on the marginal prime cost curve. For there is no reason for excess capacity in divisible equipment. Thus since net investment is not zero at all times, Kalecki's theory requires us to assume that all of this net investment is of a type such that it cannot be imputed to any given derived increase in output, i.e. that investment is always lumpy! This on the whole seems a very large assumption to make, and Kalecki certainly provides no proof for this proposition. Unless such proof is forthcoming the marginal cost curve on which output and price policies are based may include a large element of non-labour of raw material costs.

But let us assume that it has been proven that there are significant indivisibilities in capital goods. What determines the entrepreneur's demand for these? Kalecki is not very helpful on this topic. He maintains that to any 'type' of equipment there corresponds a 'normal price' of output, i.e. that price which covers all costs plus normal profits. The equilibrium 'type' of equipment is that type the 'normal price' for which is lowest, and the normal use of that equipment is that use which yields normal profits. If for any reason profits exceed normal (given the degree of monopoly) this will

> 'attract new entries into the industry and . . . its capital will rise in relation to sales . . . and this will go on up to the point where the rate of profit in the industry falls to normal'.[5]

It is seen that Kalecki never speaks of the amount invested or the quantity of capital employed, but only the 'type' of equipment used. We need not quarrel with this since the 'amount of capital' is in any case an ambiguous term. But supposing the equilibrium type of equipment has been installed, does Kalecki's theory imply that once installed our entrepreneur will never instal any more, i.e. does he suggest that in the absence of innovations etc., any given entrepreneur will always have zero net investment? This presumably is what is meant by permanent excess capacity. But who then undertakes the investments which we know to be undertaken in the boom? Kalecki presumably would have to argue that either a) excess capacity is exhausted and producers are on the upward sloping part of their marginal prime costs curve in which case his theory breaks down, or b) that all investment undertaken in the boom is by new entrants into the industry attracted by super-normal profits arising from falling average overhead costs and a constant (or rising) degree of monopoly, and this is patently untrue.

Kalecki's theory thus seems to apply only to an economy with zero net investment, that is to say it appears to be a depression theory of distribution. It is true that if there is excess capacity, and equipment is indivisible, the marginal cost of output will equal marginal prime costs and that these may remain constant. But as long as there is positive net investment, some producers at least will be on the upward rising part of the prime cost curve, i.e. some producers at least will have exhausted their excess capacity.[6] For as long as prime costs are constant, there will be no incentive for producers to invest, except by those attracted into the industry. Since investment does take place in the boom and since not all of this investment is undertaken by new entrants we must conclude that Kalecki's theory does not explain the distribution of income in an economy with positive net investment.

It may perhaps be argued that producers will invest before their excess capacity is exhausted because they expect an increase in demand. This of course may be so and producers may thus avoid rising marginal prime costs. But as we have argued in the previous chapter, given that there are reaction lags, given that it takes time to produce more investment goods and given that there will be a production lag of output, this seems extremely unlikely. But in any case dynamic considerations, implied by elastic expectations, will affect Kalecki's argument in a number of ways which we shall discuss presently.

In a depression (or stationary state) Kalecki's theory is far more likely to be correct. For then, for one thing, there will be excess capacity either because of the imperfections of the market or because too much was invested in the boom. We have already noted in the previous chapter that in a situation such as this the marginal productivity theory and theorems derived from it are not at all useful in analysing the distribution of income. Subject to certain modifications to be discussed, Kalecki's theory seems to describe this situation as well as can be hoped at this level of abstraction.

But we have up to now taken it for granted a) that equipment is indivisible and b) that this must always lead to excess capacity. But this assumption is in curious contrast to Kalecki's statement that new entrants will come into an industry until 'normal' profits are earned. It has been shown by the monopolistic competition theorists that an industry will be in equilibrium (i.e. profits normal) when the average cost curve (including normal profit) of each firm is tangential to the downwards sloping demand curve, i.e. when there is excess capacity. But surely if equipment is highly indivisible[7] normal profits will not be established. All that can be said is that there is a range of profits compatible with no firm entering or leaving the industry.

But if this is all that is meant by normal profit, the equilibrium of the industry is compatible with an upwards sloping average cost curve (excluding profit) i.e. with zero excess capacity. The fact is, that the greater the indivisibility of equipment, the greater the protection a firm enjoys from the entry of rivals.[8] Therefore Kalecki's view on this is difficult to understand. I quote him in full:

> 'It may be asked how is it possible for surplus capacity to exist in the long-run equilibrium without inducing firms to curtail their plant. The answer is that large-scale economies prevent the firms from reducing their plant below a certain limit, a state of affairs described by those writers who have shown that imperfect competition must cause equipment in the long run to be used below the "optimum point".'

Does this mean that Kalecki in fact assumes a high divisibility of equipment? If that is so then presumably entrepreneurs will equate marginal cost including the cost of extra equipment and not marginal prime cost to marginal revenue? This in fact is assumed by most writers on this topic. If he does not mean that, how can he continue to assume that there will always be excess capacity? It is clear that on *a priori* theoretical grounds, Kalecki must either drop the assumption of normal profit (uniquely determined) in which case there is no *a priori* proof of excess capacity (falling average costs) or he can continue to assume normal profits in which case equipment must be fairly divisible and thus producers will determine output and price with reference to marginal total and not to marginal prime costs.

Of course the facts may show that a) equipment is indivisible and b) that there is excess capacity. This possibility is not excluded by our theoretical considerations. All that is maintained here is that the latter do not unambiguously imply that this is so. But in any case empirical workers on this subject are not agreed on this point. This is hardly surprising when it is remembered a) how definitional many of the problems to be investigated are, e.g. what is meant by excess capacity? and b) that constantly changing techniques and the lack of proper cost accounting make quantitative analysis extremely hazardous.

As far as theoretical analysis is concerned our conclusion that Kalecki's theory is best applied to the theory of distribution in a depression when there is *unwanted* excess capacity is thus confirmed by these considerations.

2 Let us now turn to Kalecki's second basic assumption that marginal overhead cost is negligible when the amount of equipment used is constant. This, as has been pointed out by a number of writers, neglects user cost. Once again we have no hesitation in agreeing that the latter will be negligibly small in a depression. But will that be true when incomes and prices are rising?

We have noted under 1) that producers may invest in advance of increases in demand. If this is so then expectations will be elastic and incomes and probably prices will be expected to rise. Clearly user cost will now increase sharply and will have to be included in the marginal prime cost curve, and therefore the latter will rise. To this it has been objected that 'it is very doubtful whether actual business executives do treat the depreciation of their fixed equipment in the theoretical rational manner'.[9] This objection however is irrelevant. Either we follow Kalecki in assuming that business men always maximise their money profit or we don't. If we don't then we have also no reason to assume any type of marginal cost to be equal to marginal revenue. Thus we see yet again that Kalecki's theory tends to break down when incomes are expanding, i.e. when there is positive net investment, and that it is best applied to a depression economy.

3 We now turn to the question of whether the 'average degree of monopoly' is a meaningful concept.

It is open to doubt whether the degree of monopoly in fact measures the extent to which competition in the normal sense of the word is absent. Kalecki for instance assumes, as we have seen, that there is 'free entry' into each industry, and that is not what is normally associated with monopoly in everyday language. Originally the degree of monopoly was a concept of welfare economics only – showing the extent of the divergence of prices from the optimum price[10] (equal to marginal cost). It thus had a purely formal meaning and implied perfect competition as the norm for which society should aim. But perfect competition is not, as has been pointed out, competition at all in any normal sense of the word, for it postulates a world populated by mechanical producers who never reduce or increase price, never advertise and never do any of the things associated with competition.[11] It is true they enter an industry when profits exceed normal, but so do Kalecki's producers.

The term would therefore best be dropped, especially as it has led to some confusion – including on the part of Kalecki. Instead of speaking of the degree of monopoly we should simply use elasticities of demand curves, for that is all that the degree of monopoly measures.

This would make it easier to avoid such propositions as that put forward by Kalecki that the degree of monopoly has increased over the last seventy five years or so, meaning that the elasticities of demand curves facing producers on the average have diminished. I don't think there is any econometrician in the world today who would be prepared to prove this. What Kalecki clearly has in mind is the increase in the degree of concentration of industry. But this is perfectly compatible with an increase in the elasticities of the demand curves.

Again, what is meant by the 'degree of oligopoly' which he nowhere defines? If oligopolistic demand curves are kinked, the degree of oligopoly can clearly not be expressed as an inverse of the elasticity of this curve. If however the degree of oligopoly is defined as the extent to which the marginal revenue curve is discontinuous at any given equilibrium output, then the degree of oligopoly will only determine the limits within which the distribution of income must lie.

When we have stripped the concept of its rather tendentious implications we are left with the following proposition. If there is excess capacity, if marginal overhead costs are zero and if producers maximise their money profits, then in equilibrium the ratio of average to marginal revenue will coincide with the ratio of price to average cost. The greater this equilibrium ratio the smaller will be the share of wages. If we grant all the assumptions (and we have seen that in many cases we cannot) then this is undoubtedly correct. As long however as the degree of monopoly is regarded as exogenously given, this will not be very helpful for unless we know how it will change when certain parameters of the system change, we will be unable to predict the effect of such changes on the share of wages.

III

To sum up we conclude that:

1 Kalecki's theory is useful in analysing the depression distribution of

income (when there is unwanted excess capacity), but is not very helpful when net investment is positive, for then there is no reason why his basic assumptions should hold.

2 Kalecki's theory has not been proven on theoretical grounds to apply to stationary states with zero net investment or disinvestment. For this will depend on whether equipment is in fact indivisible and whether producers are in fact on the downward falling part of their average (total) cost curves. This cannot be shown to be true *a priori* for we cannot assume free entry when there are significant indivisibilities.

3 The 'average degree of monopoly' is not a measure of any of the attributes normally associated with monopoly. A change in the degree of monopoly therefore need not imply a change in the degree of concentration of industry or any increase in any other index of monopoly power.

4 Kalecki's theory cannot deal adequately with oligopoly.

To these conclusions we may now add that

5 Kalecki stipulates a supply curve of entrepreneurship by speaking of 'normal' profit but says nothing about this curve.

6 Kalecki's theory is static and ignores all lags. Therefore in common with the theory discussed in the previous chapter it gives us less help in determining what the share of wages will be at any one moment of time than in showing what this share would be if equilibrium (under certain assumptions) were established.

This concludes our analysis of Kalecki's theory, although we shall return to it and some of Kalecki's opinions later on in this book. But first we shall make an attempt to formulate a macro-economic, short run theory of the share of wages, by using both the theories discussed in this and the previous chapter, and by taking account of some further factors which will influence the equilibrium share of wages in the short run.

Chapter 3
A simple model

It is the purpose of this chapter to present a simple, short run, macroeconomic theory of distribution. In the model to be analysed, we shall not only take account of the influence of marginal productivity and the 'degree of monopoly' on the share of wages, but shall also stipulate an aggregate supply function of output based on the assumption that entrepreneurs maximise an index of utility rather than their money profits.

It is well known that this assumption interpreted with the greatest generality can only lead to a number of classificatory results, for while the sign of the substitution term is always unambiguous that of the income term is not.[1] To avoid this classification we have assumed the entrepreneur's preference function to be of a particular form. This is equivalent to assuming the income term always to be of a certain sign. This assumption has the advantage of enabling us to formulate definite propositions which can be tested against actual observed behaviour of entrepreneurs.

Making use of the above assumptions we shall derive an aggregate supply curve of output as a function of the net profit margin (rate of profit on output). We shall show that in certain circumstances the relation between net profit margin and the share of wages is linear, so that the aggregate supply of output can equally well be expressed as a function of the share of wages. Making use of the relation between the share of wages and the propensity to consume and between investment and aggregate supply, we shall derive an aggregate demand curve. The equilibrium share of wages will then be that which equates aggregate supply and aggregate demand.

I

If there is a perfect (or near perfect) capital market, then at any one moment of time there will be some individuals on the margin of entrepreneurship and some entrepreneurs on the margin of expanding their output, or of entering some market other than their present one, or producing some commodities they are not producing already. We shall assume that the factor restraining those individuals from becoming entrepreneurs, or expanding their output etc., is uncertainty or, if we like, the general disutility of production. An individual entrepreneur is therefore in equilibrium, not when marginal profit is zero, but when the marginal rate of transformation of output into profit is equal to his (subjective) marginal rate of substitution of output for profit. Whether or not this equilibrium is achieved on the basis of mathematical expectations and whether individuals 'quantify' their subjective feeling of uncertainty, or whether they estimate 'potential surprise', is irrelevant to the present discussion. All that our assumption comes to is that uncertainty tends to restrain individuals from enterprise and a high rate of return to induce them towards it.

We shall assume that entrepreneurs always expect the present state of affairs, i.e. price, demand, costs, etc. to continue over their economic horizon. We also assume that there is no taxation and that the prices of the goods entrepreneurs consume are constant. We can then write the utility function of our entrepreneur as

$$U = U(P, Ot, E, \eta), \quad (3.1)$$

where P is profit, O is outlay and t is the average rate of turnover, E is the amount of the entrepreneur's own labour, and η is a parameter measuring residual uncertainties undertaken which are independent of O and t. U is an increasing function of P and a diminishing function of O, t and E. If we further assume that there are only two factors besides the entrepreneur, labour and capital and that they all three vary directly with output, and if η is constant, we can rewrite 3.1 as

$$U = U(P, X), \quad (3.2)$$

where X is output.

Given the demand and cost schedules facing the entrepreneur we can write

$$P = P(X). \quad (3.3)$$

Hence, maximising 3.2 subject to 3.3 we obtain the equilibrium condition

$$\frac{U_X}{U_P} = -P'(X). \quad (3.4)$$

(The suffixes denote differentiation.)

But now a difficulty arises. If at any one moment of time there is a given stock of capital, then if output falls below full capacity output, no new outlay on capital goods needs to be undertaken. Hence to produce such a lower output, the amount of funds to be invested per unit of output diminishes and their rate of turnover increases. For simplicity's sake, we shall assume that for output below capacity, the marginal disutility of production is zero, or if we like the marginal utility of profits increases very sharply relatively to the marginal disutility of producing. For then the only uncertainty undertaken in producing is due to the funds spent on labour and their turnover is very high.

Making this assumption, equation 3.2 must be regarded as applicable only to those situations for which $X > X_0$ (where X_0 is full capacity output). The equations 3.2 and 3.3 are plotted in the diagram (figure 3).

Given the demand and minimum cost conditions, OP, the profit curve, is uniquely determined. $I_0 I_0$ is an indifference curve between output and profit. This curve will shift for any change in η or t. OM is the equilibrium

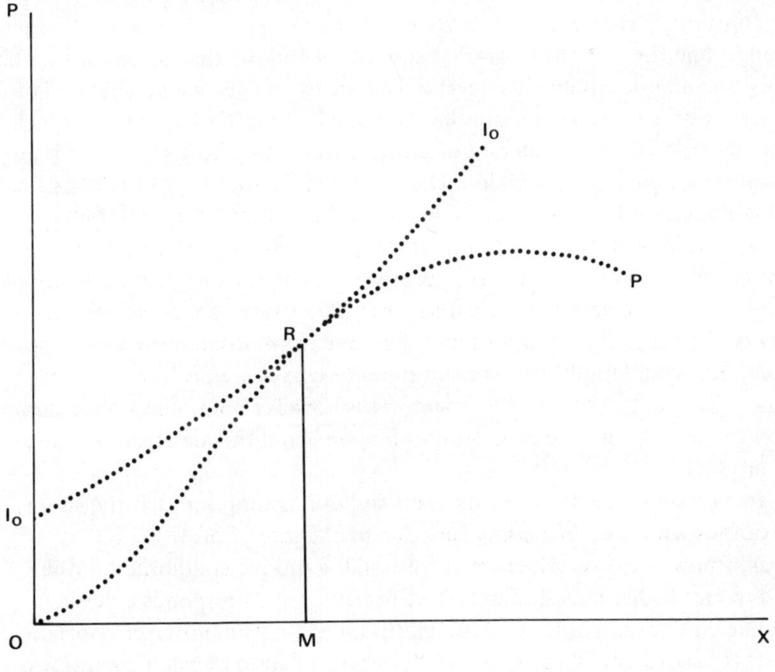

figure 3

output and the slope of the straight line OR (not drawn) measures the rate of profit on output.

We now make our special assumption concerning the entrepreneur's preference function: it will be assumed that the income term is zero, i.e. that the above indifference curves are vertical projections of each other.[2] This assumption rules out a backward rising supply curve of output and it implies a constant marginal utility of income. Backward rising supply curves of output, except in one-man businesses such as small-scale farming, seem rare and can safely be ruled out. Constant marginal utility of income leads to logical difficulties, and is assumed here only for the sake of simplicity.[3] In general our propositions will hold whenever the income term is positive provided we can assume that the marginal disutility of producing at constant costs and given expectations increases faster than the marginal utility of income (which will always be true as long as the marginal utility of income is either constant or decreasing).

From the assumptions the following propositions can be derived. Provided that any shift in the demand curve is a horizontal iso-elastic shift, the relationship between profit per unit of output and marginal profit will be constant.[4] Hence the profit OP curves will be projections of each other along a line through the origin.[5] From this it follows that there corresponds only one unique equilibrium level of output to any given (average) rate of profit. For if there were more than one level of equilibrium output which corresponded to any given rate of profit, this would imply that there is an indifference curve $I_1 I_1$ which to the north east or south west of R has the same slope as $I_0 I_0$ at R. This however would contradict our assumption.

It is easily seen that this result will still hold even when the income term is not zero but positive as long as we assume the marginal disutility of producing to increase faster than the marginal utility of income. For if to any profit per unit of output more than one equilibrium output were possible, this would imply that the indifference curves are projections of each other along a line through the origin. This however contradicts our assumption concerning the marginal utility of income and the marginal disutility of producing.

It is further clear from the diagram and our assumption that the supply of output will be an increasing function of the rate of profit.[6] To any equilibrium rate of profit there corresponds a unique equilibrium output, and to any higher equilibrium rate of profit there corresponds a higher unique equilibrium output. Also, given our assumption of given constant costs (i.e. constant factor ratios and prices) and given demand conditions, there corresponds a unique share of wages to any given rate of profit. Since the share of wages is inversely related to $\frac{P}{X}$ (the rate of profit), the supply of output will be a diminishing function of $\frac{W}{X}$ (where W is the total wage bill).

If we now assume that relative prices of outputs remain constant, i.e. that entrepreneurs' utility functions are similar and that they are faced with the same proportionate increases in demand and are all producing under constant returns, then we can draw an aggregate supply curve of output. (These assumptions of course will not be fulfilled and we shall drop them in a subsequent chapter.)

The aggregate supply curve on these assumptions is plotted in figure 4. Given any value of $\frac{W}{X}$ we can read off the corresponding equilibrium value of X which is compatible with it. Or to put it differently, since in equilibrium demand must equal supply, the supply curve shows what the demand would have to be in order that any value of $\frac{W}{X}$ should be an equi-

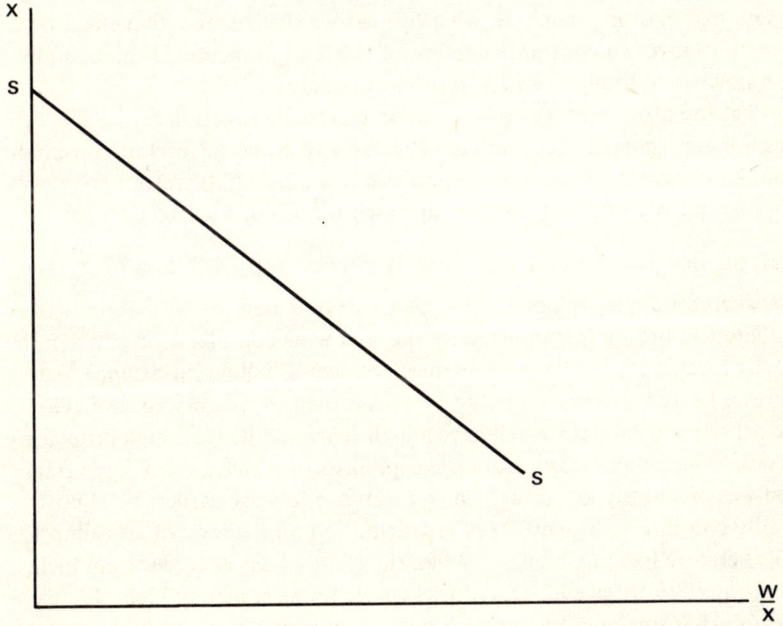

figure 4

librium value. In order to complete our analysis we must therefore examine the forces determining aggregate demand.

II

Aggregate demand is, assuming a closed economy, the sum of consumption and investment demand. We shall consider each in turn.

Consumption demand is a function of the level of income, the distribution of income, the rate of interest, the volume of real cash balances, and some average of previous incomes. In what follows we shall assume that the influence of the rate of interest and the volume of real cash balances on the level of consumption is small. Moreover, since our analysis is static we shall ignore the time-lag of changes in consumption habits which is implied by the term 'average of previous incomes'. We are then left with two main determining factors: the level and distribution of income.

For our purposes it is immaterial whether the propensity to consume is an increasing, constant, or diminishing function of the level of income. Such data as are available (although very scanty) seem to indicate that the propensity to consume over normal times does not vary much with the absolute level of income.[7] In what follows we shall assume that the propensity to save is a constant function of the level of income. This assumption however is in no way necessary to our analysis.

That the propensity to consume is an increasing function of the share of wages seems generally recognised. The curve relating the level of consumption out of any given income to the share of wages will therefore be upward sloping. We shall further assume, although this is not necessary to our analysis, that the slope of this curve is steepest for low values of $\frac{W}{X}$ and less steep for higher values.

This assumption is supported by the following considerations. When the share of wages is low, i.e. wage-earners are near or below subsistence,[8] an increase in that share is unlikely to increase their propensity to save. On the other hand capitalists will have a high share and hence a high propensity to save. One pound taken from the capitalists of which a fairly large fraction was previously saved, will on transference to wage-earners be almost wholly consumed. The effect of redistribution on the level of consumption will therefore be at its highest. When the share of wages is relatively high, the propensity to save of wage-earners will also be relatively high. Firstly because subsistence needs are no longer so pressing and secondly because savings will become a social desideratum as employed workers acquire middle class habits. Capitalists on the other hand will now have a lower propensity to save, since, except in the very long run, capitalists' consumption habits appear to be fairly stable. The effect of redistribution in favour of wage-earners on the level of consumption, in this situation, will therefore be relatively small.

For convenience of diagrammatic exposition the curves of savings rather than consumption are plotted in figure 5. Each of the SS curves relates to a given level of income.

Investment demand is a function of the rate of interest, the rate of change in income and the stock of capital, and some residual factors which we assume constant. Any investment demand schedule is only valid as long as the stock of capital is constant. Any change in the latter will shift the former. We must therefore start with a given stock of capital, and since we have assumed that there is no excess capacity, a given level of income. An investment demand schedule must therefore be understood to be valid only in the short run – or to put it differently, our analysis applies to short period flow equilibrium only.

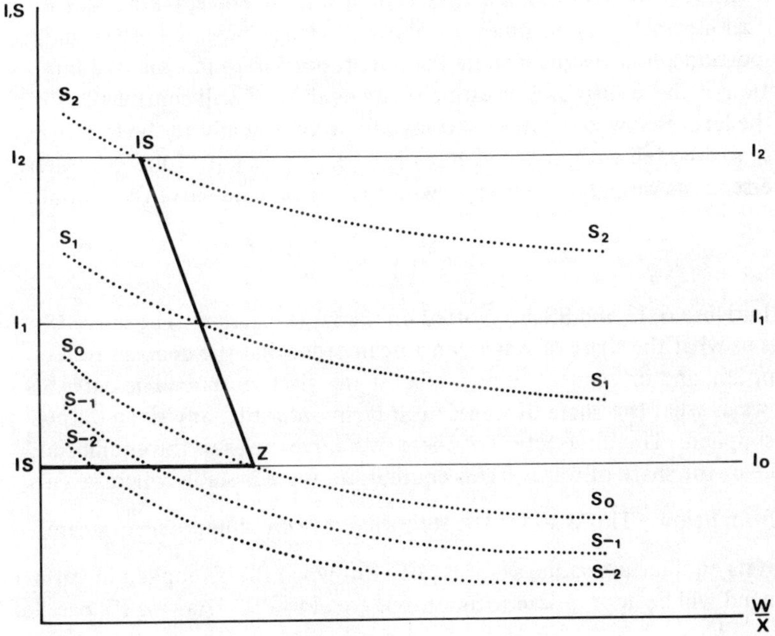

figure 5

Thus starting with any given level of income = X_0, investment will rise in more than proportion to income for incomes greater than X_0, owing to the working of the accelerator. This does not mean that we are introducing dynamic considerations into the static analysis; we are *not* allowing for any lags. All we wish to imply is that starting with any given stock of capital and income and zero excess capacity, an increase in income will call forth a more than proportionate increase in investment demand. For incomes less than X_0, (remembering that at X_0 there is only autonomous and replacement investment) investment will remain approximately constant.

We shall assume that investment demand is interest-inelastic. While probably not completely true, this appears sufficiently so for this level of abstraction. Lastly, our investment demand schedule must be understood to show the amount that would be invested if any given level of income were produced. It is therefore a purely physically determined quantity (it will be remembered that we are assuming constant factor ratios) and takes no account of expectations. Being physically determined it is independent of the share of wages. The investment curves are plotted in figure 5, $I_0 I_0$ being the investment curve appropriate to the level of income X_0 we start out with (i.e. representing the given capital stock). Since, taking X_0 as normal income, when incomes rise above it savings increase in the same proportion and investment more than in proportion to income, the intersection of the savings and investment curves above Z will continually shift to the left. Below Z the intersections will be continually to the left of Z since savings fall with income while investment does not. Joining all these intersections we obtain a curve IS which is the demand curve for output.

III

In figure 6, IS and SS are plotted on the same diagram. The curve IS tells us what the share of wages must be in order that the demand for consumption and investment should exhaust any given output. The curve SS shows us what the share of wages must be in order that any given output be supplied. The intersection of these two curves gives us the equilibrium value of the share of wages. This equilibrium value is stable when SS cuts IS from below. This is so for the following reasons. Suppose $\frac{W}{X}$ greater than its equilibrium value, say it is OR. But when PR is supplied investment demand will be appropriate to an output equal to PR. Drawing PT parallel to the $\frac{W}{X}$ axis to intersect IS at G, we find the share of wages at which

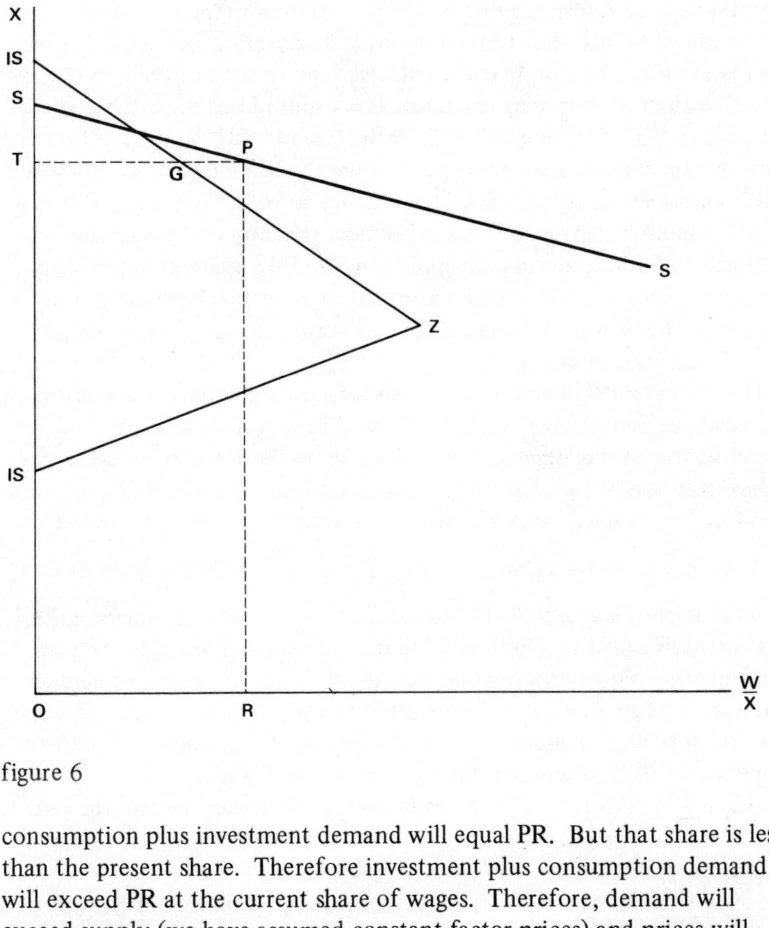

figure 6

consumption plus investment demand will equal PR. But that share is less than the present share. Therefore investment plus consumption demand will exceed PR at the current share of wages. Therefore, demand will exceed supply (we have assumed constant factor prices) and prices will rise and real wages and thus $\frac{W}{X}$ fall. Similarly for any value of $\frac{W}{X}$ below the equilibrium value, savings will exceed investment, there will be excess supply and prices will fall and real wages and hence $\frac{W}{X}$ rise.[9]

Any fall in money wages will tend to shift the supply curve. The average rate of turnover of capital will be increased, or reduced, according as the elasticity of substitution, σ, is greater or less than unity, for the elasticity of substitution will determine the change in the ratio of total wages to non-wage payments (the latter being assumed to have a lower rate of turnover).

In so far as uncertainty is a diminishing function of t (the rate of turnover), the supply curve will shift to the right or left according as σ is greater or less than unity. The supply curve will also tend to shift to the right, because the amount of money capital used per unit of output will be reduced, irrespective of σ. Hence if $\sigma > 1$, SS will certainly shift to the right for the above reason and the share of wages will tend to diminish. This may seem odd if we remember what was said about this topic in Chapter 1. But in a macro-economic analysis we must remember that any increase in the willingness of entrepreneurs to supply output also implies an increase in investment demand. Since this is assumed to increase more than in proportion to the increase in output, the equilibrium share of wages, other things being equal, must decline.

The IS curve will however tend to shift to the right since less investment is needed per unit of output. This will tend to increase the share of wages. Therefore everything depends on the relative shifts of the two curves. No *a priori* solution of the effect of wage reductions on the share of wages can therefore be obtained. Exactly the same applies to a rise in money wages.

A rise in the degree of monopoly $\left(\frac{1}{e}\right)$ associated with any given output, i.e. a fall in the elasticity of the individual demand curves facing producers, costs being assumed constant, will reduce the marginal profit on output. Remembering our assumptions concerning the entrepreneurial preference function, the supply curve will be shifted to the left and the share of wages will therefore be increased. A fall in the degree of monopoly will shift the supply curve to the right and diminish the share of wages.

Changes in entrepreneurial expectations, as well as changes in the general degree of certainty (however defined) associated with any given situation will also shift the supply curve.

Lastly we may note some special cases which will be examined in more detail in the next chapter.

1 If the marginal disutility of producing and the marginal utility of income are both constant, all our other assumptions being given, SS will be vertical.[10] The share of wages is then fully determined independently of demand conditions.

2 If the amount saved changes with income as the amount invested does, the IS curve will be vertical. This is what economists have called neutral equilibrium. The use of the supply curve as long as 1) does not hold, however, enables us to determine equilibrium output. The share of wages in this case is uniquely determined by the demand conditions.

3 Whenever oligopoly and/or price leadership are significant the profit

curve of figure 3 will become discontinuous. This will imply that over certain ranges the supply curve will be vertical, i.e. will exhibit a kink. This kink however must be in the vicinity of the intersection of the normal supply curve with the demand curve. For the further away it is from the latter the greater will be the strain on the discipline of the group. (See post.)

IV

In the model just outlined we have made very many simplifying assumptions which, while permissible for a short run flow equilibrium analysis, make it of little use for any other type of work. On the other hand we believe that it has proved helpful in understanding the implications of modern (static) macro-economics for the theory of distribution.

Of course much of the validity of the model depends on the validity of the assumptions concerning entrepreneurial utility functions and these will be re-examined in the next chapter. But they certainly do not seem different from those made by other authors (frequently in footnotes), and though perhaps we have oversimplified the problem, the general direction of change is likely to be correct.

But a further difficulty may arise. We are so used to assume that if *ex ante* investment exceeds *ex ante* savings, incomes will rise until *ex ante* investment and savings are equal, that the above analysis may appear out of step with modern theory. But this is not so. For one thing the assumption of constant prices usually made need not be correct, and we have in fact postulated that it is not. Secondly, if investment demand increases with incomes (such that the propensity to invest plus the propensity to consume is greater than unity), then there is no reason why equilibrium should be reached. Again, the assumption that the propensity to invest plus the propensity to consume is less than unity need not be correct. In fact this will only be so *ex post*. For starting with a given stock of capital, investment demand will increase more than in proportion to income. Since we have assumed the rate of interest either constant or to have no effect on investment demand, it will be changes in the share of wages which will perform the function of the rate of interest in bringing about equilibrium by reducing the propensity to consume. Therefore just as in the Keynesian model there is one rate of interest for each level of income which will equate *ex ante* savings to *ex ante* investment, so there is one share of wages (in our theory) to each level of income which will perform the same function. Our theory therefore differs from the normal Keynesian model in that it explicitly postulates that the burden of adjustment will fall on the share of wages and not the rate of interest. This will be discussed in greater detail in later chapters.

Chapter 4
Some structural problems

Up to now we have dealt in terms of aggregates, i.e. aggregate income and the aggregate share of wages. In this chapter we examine some of the problems concealed by this approach. In particular, attention will be drawn to the following facts.

1 The demand for consumption goods will be a function of the share of wages in terms of these goods, while the supply of investment goods will be a function of the share of wages in the investment goods industry measured in terms of investment goods, and the supply of consumption goods will be a function of the share of wages (in terms of consumption goods) in that industry. More than one definition of the share of wages is therefore involved.

2 Because of 1) the share of wages (however expressed) in the index of the share for the whole economy will not only vary with the level, but also with the structure of income. This is especially important when considering the share of wages in the trade cycle.[1]

This chapter makes no attempt to deal with the aggregation problem in full, i.e. it does not aim at splitting the economy into all its constituent parts. Instead we shall continue to work with the sub-aggregates of consumption and investment goods.

I

The easiest way of dealing with the two main problems outlined above is to construct a simple mathematical model of the economy, in which the splitting of output into consumption and investment goods is made explicit.

In equilibrium the real wage of labour in any one industry is equal to the marginal product of labour multiplied by what we shall call an 'exploitation coefficient'. In current analysis, the latter is identified with the degree of monopoly, i.e. the marginal product is multiplied by $\left(1 - \frac{1}{e}\right)$ (where e is the elasticity of demand). Since however we are taking account of entrepreneurial uncertainty discounts, our exploitation coefficient will be greater than $\left(1 - \frac{1}{e}\right)$.

If we denote by the subscript i the investment, and by the subscript c, the consumption industry, we can write the following four equations:

$$\text{(supply of investment)} \quad I^s = I(N_i), \qquad (4.1)$$

$$\text{(supply of consumption goods)} \quad C^s = C(N_c), \qquad (4.2)$$

$$\frac{w}{p_i} = I'(N_i)t_i\,, \qquad (4.3)$$

$$\frac{w}{p_c} = C'(N_c)\epsilon_c, \qquad (4.4)$$

where N_i and N_c are the amount of labour employed in I (investment) and C (consumption goods industries) respectively, $\frac{w}{p_i}$ is the real wage of labour in I in terms of I, and $\frac{w}{p_c}$ is the real wage of labour in C in terms of C, ϵ_i and ϵ_c are the exploitation coefficients in I and C, and I′ and C′ denote first differentials, i.e. marginal products. Equations 4.1 and 4.2 are production functions on the assumption that the stock of capital is given, while 4.3 and 4.4 show the equilibrium values of $\frac{w}{p_i}$ and $\frac{w}{p_c}$.

Making use of the assumption of previous chapters that the uncertainty of producing output is increasing with output and assuming all demand elasticities constant, we can write two further equations.

$$\epsilon_i = \epsilon_i(I) \quad (\epsilon_i < 1), \qquad (4.5)$$

$$\epsilon_c = \epsilon_c(C) \quad (\epsilon_c < 1), \qquad (4.6)$$

where both ϵ_i and ϵ_c are assumed diminishing functions of I and C. We next define the share of wages $\left(\frac{W}{Y}\right)_c$ in terms of C by the following equation.

$$\left(\frac{W}{Y}\right)_c = \frac{RN_iI'(N_i)\epsilon_i + N_cC'(N_c)\epsilon_c}{RI(N_i) + C(N_c)}, \qquad (4.7)$$

where R is defined as

$$R = \left(\frac{I'(N_i)\epsilon_i}{C'(N_c)\epsilon_c}\right). \quad (4.8)$$

It is clear from 4.7 that $\left(\frac{W}{Y}\right)_c$ will vary with 1) total output, 2) the ratio of investment to total output and the ratio of consumption to total output and 3) with R which by 4.8 is equal to the ratio of the price of investment goods (p_i) to the price of consumption goods (p_c) (assuming the money wage the same in I and C).

Having defined $\left(\frac{W}{Y}\right)_c$ we can now write the demand for consumption goods C^d as a function of $\left(\frac{W}{Y}\right)_c$ and the level of income Y. We have

$$C^d = F\left[\left(\frac{W}{Y}\right)_c, Y\right]. \quad (4.9)$$

The demand for investment goods I^d in this simple static approach will be regarded as a function of the level of income only. But we postulate that $Y > Y_0$ the full capacity output. We therefore have

$$I^d = f(Y) \quad (Y > Y_0). \quad (4.10)$$

For equilibrium the demand for investment goods must equal their supply and the demand for consumption goods must also equal their supply. We thus have

$$I(N_i) = f(Y), \quad (4.11)$$

$$C(N_c) = F\left[\left(\frac{W}{Y}\right)_c, Y\right]. \quad (4.12)$$

Also income is defined as the sum of investment and consumption, i.e.

$$Y = C + I. \quad (4.13)$$

The system 4.1 to 4.13 is fully determinate having the thirteen unknowns,

$I^s, I^d, C^s, C^d, \frac{w}{p_i}, \frac{w}{p_c}, \epsilon_i, \epsilon_c, N_i, N_c, \left(\frac{W}{Y}\right)_c$, R and Y. It should be noted, however, that in spite of this it is not a fully satisfactory system, since it is entirely in real terms, taking no account of absolute price levels. This in a full analysis would lead to difficulties,[2] but here we are concerned with the effects of changes in *relative* prices and output and for this purpose the above model is most suitable.

It is now seen however that an increase in the supply of output may well be accompanied by a fall in the share of wages in terms of consumption goods. Let us suppose for the moment that there are constant returns to labour. Then $I(N_i)$ increases in the same proportion as N_i and $C(N_c)$ in the same proportion as N_c. The marginal products of N_i and N_c also remain constant. Therefore any change in $\left(\frac{W}{Y}\right)_c$ (see equation 4.7) must be due to a change in the exploitation coefficients ϵ_i and ϵ_c, or a change in the composition of output. In the previous chapter we also assumed that ϵ_i and ϵ_c would change in the same proportion, and neglected the effect of a change in the composition of output.

Now ϵ_i and ϵ_c are both less than unity. If now as incomes expand ϵ_i falls by less than ϵ_c, the composition of output remaining the same, then R (see 4.8) will increase and hence the share of wages may increase. But more important still, if the composition of output changes so that say N_i increases by more than in proportion to output and N_c by less, and if R remaining constant the marginal product of labour in I is greater than in C, then the share of wages may again increase.

Thus even though the marginal uncertainty of production is increasing with output, the aggregate supply curve may be an increasing function of the share of wages in terms of consumption goods.

But beyond possibly altering the shape of our aggregate supply curve our main conclusions of the previous chapter are unaffected.

For in the above model if we start with a given level of income the share of wages $\left(\frac{W}{Y}\right)_c$ is in the first instance determined by the production functions and the exploitation coefficients. But we cannot, as is so frequently done in current literature, stop here. The share of wages thus determined will call forth a certain demand for consumption goods which together with the demand for investment goods (as a function of the given income) may exceed the income we started out with. But when incomes now rise the exploitation coefficients as well as the marginal products of labour may change and thus the share of wages may also change. The equilibrium share of wages $\left(\frac{W}{Y}\right)_c$ is therefore that share which, when established, will cause people in the role of consumers (in the widest sense) to allocate their expenditure between investment and consumption goods in the same proportion as producers allocate their resources between these two and cause demand and supply to be equal in both markets.

It is seen that taking explicit account of relative prices does not materially alter our conclusions of previous chapters. It is however important to remember that any shift in any of the functions may affect the share of wages even if aggregate income as the sum of investment and consumption goods remains constant.

Lastly we may note that our model can easily take account of the influence of the rate of interest on investment (and possibly consumption) demand. By putting the rate of interest into these two demand functions, and adding a liquidity preference equation (which can include the effect of changes in the distribution of income on the demand for money), our system is still fully determinate. It is clear on general grounds and from our discussion in the previous chapter that in so far as the rate of interest varies and in so far as it is effective in reducing both investment and consumption demand, it will exert a dampening effect on fluctuations in the share of wages. This is because a part of the burden of bringing about equilibrium between aggregate supply and aggregate demand will now fall on the rate of interest, so that variations in the share of wages will be less than they would otherwise have been. In terms of figure 5 in the previous chapter, it implies that the IS curve will be steeper than it would otherwise have been.

Chapter 5
Two special cases

The purpose of this chapter is to examine some special cases which modify the conclusions reached at the end of the previous chapter. The following problems will come up for consideration:

1 the possibility of a vertical supply curve and
2 the effect of oligopoly on our conclusions.

I

The supply curve of output will be vertical in a stationary state, provided there are constant returns to scale. For when incomes are stationary and net investment (and saving) zero, there is no uncertainty of production since all decisions are routine decisions. It is for this sort of economic system that the current theories of distribution are most appropriate. The share of wages in the national income is now determined by marginal productivity and the 'degree of monopoly' only. But the case of a stationary state is not very interesting – it has, after all, never yet been reached, and we therefore need not concern ourselves greatly with this problem.

But there is another set of assumptions which will lead us to expect a vertical supply curve, namely that of a constant marginal disutility of production. This is implied by the popular 'full cost' principle of pricing.[1] According to the latter, entrepreneurs always charge a price such that their average net profit margin remains (approximately) constant.

If this is correct then once again the share of wages is determined independently of the level of demand. Unfortunately however no one has been able to say how the net profit margin is determined. Moreover, the evidence which proponents of this principle have collected seems at best to show that over certain ranges of output the marginal uncertainty of production remains constant, or increases very slowly. Most of the entrepreneurs interviewed seem to have argued that they operate on this principle only in 'normal' times, i.e. when demand and output are not fluctuating very much. The conventional net profit margin thus comes down to being nothing very much more than Marshallian normal profit and we would all agree that in long run equilibrium the net profit margin remains constant.

One suspects that the interviewing technique is not very well suited to an analysis of entrepreneurial behaviour. A great deal will depend on the type of question asked. Every entrepreneur is under the necessity of fixing some price when he puts his goods on the market. It is only natural that he should proceed by trial and error, always fixing a price which, for the expected output, will cover his costs and leave him some profit. But that does not mean that the final equilibrium price will be the price he fixed originally. Once equilibrium is reached and the entrepreneur is asked how the price is fixed, he tends to say that he has fixed it by finding his average costs and adding a 'fair' or 'normal' profit margin, which is true but gives us no idea of how the actual price has been arrived at.[2] Moreover, by a 'fair' profit margin all that may be meant is that it is adequate to cover the disutility of the particular output our entrepreneur is producing.

But however that may be, at present the evidence is insufficient for us to be justified in abandoning the more conventional analysis. It may well be that at any one moment of time there is, in different industries, a definite profit margin which is regarded as just or fair and that it would be bad business etiquette to earn a profit either higher or lower than that. But, one feels, and the full-cost theorists themselves imply, that this phenomenon would be most likely in oligopolistic industries. In the latter however it is not profit margins but prices which tend to be stabilised, and that is quite a different matter from our point of view.

Lastly, it is well known that profit margins have in fact fluctuated over the course of the trade cycle and so of course have prices.[3] The full cost theory as it stands at present gives us very little aid in explaining this. We feel therefore justified, at present at any rate, in regarding the full cost principle of pricing, in so far as it does not refer to oligopolistic practices and in so far as it leads to different results from the more conventional analysis, as a special case. We now turn to examine the case of oligopoly.

II

When considering the supply curve in the previous chapter we assumed that the curves facing the entrepreneur were continuous and smooth. That need not be so. If there are price agreements or in general oligopolistic market conditions, the OP curve of figure 3, chapter 3 may be kinked at a given output. That is to say an increase in output may lead to a big discrete fall in profit. This case of course corresponds to the kinked demand curve analysis of oligopoly as currently used. The problem which however remains in the latter type of approach is to determine where the kink will occur. Our method of analysis developed in the previous chapter may help us to say something more definite about this problem.

The main point of importance to note is that the difference between what would be supplied at any given value of $\left(\frac{W}{Y}\right)$ in the absence of price agreement or leadership, which we shall call the 'normal' supply, and what actually is supplied when there is such agreement etc., must not be too large. For the larger this gap the more likely is the break in the discipline of the group concerned. Thus the greater the excess of 'normal' over actual supply, the greater will be the excess of marginal profit over the marginal disutility (uncertainty) of production and the greater also is *ceteris paribus* the pressure of potential entrepreneurs to enter and for existing entrepreneurs to expand output. Similarly the greater the excess of actual over 'normal' supply the smaller will be the excess of marginal profit over the marginal disutility of production and the greater will be the pressure to contract output. This is best illustrated in the diagram (figure 7).

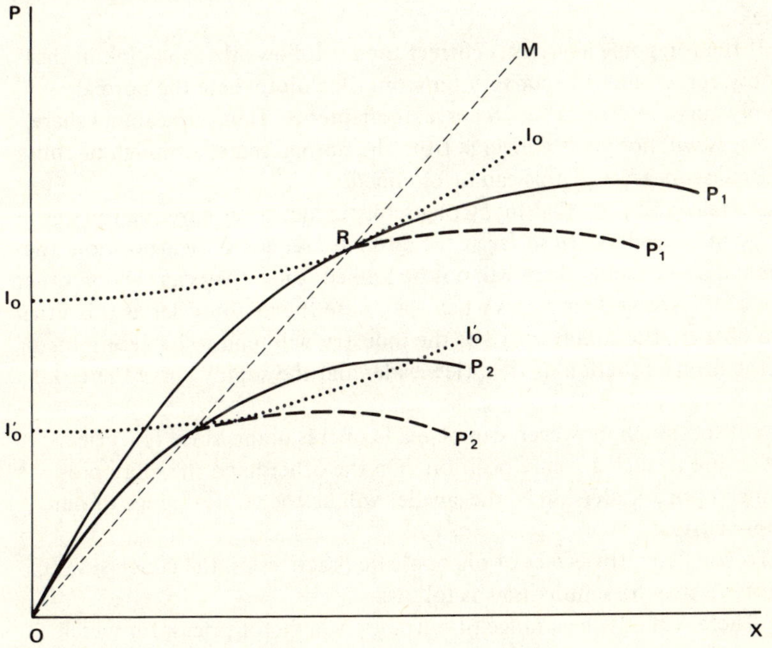

figure 7

In figure 7, $I_0 I_0$ and OP_1 are again the entrepreneur's indifference curve between output and profit, and the output-profit transformation curves respectively. These two curves are tangential at R at an average rate of profit given by the slope of OM. If now, given factor prices etc., agreement is reached to stabilise prices at that level which yields the given average rate of profit, our transformation curve will assume the slope shown by OP'_1, i.e. there will now be a kink in the curve at R. But actual output will coincide with 'normal' supply. Suppose now that our transformation curve falls such that, assuming constant costs, the kink of the lower curve also lies on OM. The lower the curve OP_2 the further to the left of our indifference map will the kink occur. But the further we move to the left, i.e. the lower output, the smaller will be the slope of our indifference curve, so that eventually one of the indifference curves will be tangential to OP'_2 to the right of the kink, i.e. the discipline of the group will break. This occurs in our figure when OP_1 has fallen to OP'_2. Therefore the greater the excess of 'normal' supply at any given values of $\left(\frac{W}{Y}\right)$ (i.e. slope of OM) over actual supply the more likely is it that the discipline of the group will break.

If the foregoing analysis is correct then it follows that the kink in the supply curve cannot occur very far from the point where the normal supply curve intersects the IS curve of chapter 3. Hence the actual share of wages will not greatly diverge from the normal share, although of course no precise measure of this can be obtained.

We may also note that many oligopolistic industries have their prices set by price leaders. In so far as the latter are secure in their position, the demand curve facing them will not be kinked, since they can rely on other producers raising their prices when they raise theirs. In so far as this situation obtains, the supply curve of the industry will tend to be determined by the utility function of the price leader and the supply curve therefore need not be kinked.

Not too much, however, can be made of this point, since few price leaders are in such a secure position. On the other hand the more pronounced price leadership is, the smaller will be the vertical range of our supply curve.

To conclude, the effect of oligopolistic practices on the conclusions of chapter 3 may be summarised as follows:

1 There will now be a range of output, given factor prices, for which there will be no change in the share of wages.

2 Given the price agreed upon, there will be a range of the share of wages

which is compatible with equilibrium.

3 The kink in the supply curve is likely to move in the same direction as the intersection of the normal supply curve with the IS curve moves.

4 The presence of oligopoly will have the minimum effect on the shape of our supply curve when price leadership is strong, and the maximum effect when price leadership is weak.

The occurrence and extent of oligopolistic practices seems to be closely connected with fluctuations in the level of activity, and we shall return to this problem again when these fluctuations are considered.

Chapter 6

The dynamics of the share of wages

In a previous chapter we have examined the conditions of equilibrium at a moment of time. It is clear that we cannot leave matters there. In our analysis we leaned heavily on the 'uncertainty principle' of profit determination and uncertainty as well as profit is essentially a dynamic phenomenon. This chapter will accordingly attempt to make a preliminary survey of some of the new problems raised by a dynamic analysis.

I

It is well known that in a stationary state, i.e. a zero rate of growth of output, uncertainty will eventually be reduced to zero. In a 'circular flow' economy there is no room for anything but routine decisions. But does not the same apply to an economy progressing at a constant rate of growth?

The answer is surely in the affirmative. Expectations are based on past happenings. The certainty with which particular expectations are held will depend on whether expectations in the past have been disappointed more often than not. If output has in fact been expanding at a constant rate in the past, entrepreneurs will tend to expect it to expand at a constant rate in the future. Each time they will find that their expectations have been fulfilled. Clearly if this continues, uncertainty will continuously decline and will eventually vanish. If this is correct then in a regular progressing economy the share of wages will be determined by the orthodox factors: the degree of monopoly, the production function and the prices of the factors of production. There is however no guarantee (or indeed likelihood) that the share so determined will result in a propensity to consume compatible with a constant rate of growth in output. A constant rate of growth in output is as fictitious as a zero rate of growth.

The above conclusions however are only correct, if not only the rate of growth in output is constant but other variables are either also constant or changing at a constant rate. We shall show in a later chapter that this is in fact not so, except in very special circumstances, and that a constant rate of growth in output will require continuous innovation on the part of the entrepreneur and that this will tend to prevent the decline of uncertainty to zero. For the moment however we accept the conclusion that the orthodox theory of distribution will apply in a regular progressing economy.

II

Since it is fairly evident that in reality we never find an economy progressing at a constant rate, this case is not very interesting, although it may help us to understand certain basic problems. Let us therefore examine the implications of an increasing (positive) rate of growth.

An increase in the rate of growth in output will tend to increase the uncertainty of production and the greater the change the greater is the increase in uncertainty likely to be. Any change in the rate of growth of output will require entrepreneurs to reinterpret the economic situation in which they are placed. The greater and more frequent the change in the rate of growth of output the greater will be the difficulty of this reassessment, the more unsettled will the economic climate be and the more reluctant, *ceteris paribus,* will entrepreneurs be to undertake new commitments. This is certainly true if we regard the 'degree of optimism' as given. In short, a changing rate of growth makes forecasts more difficult since there is no regular past experience on which to base such forecasts and hence uncertainty will tend to increase.

But there is also another reason why the willingness to produce should be a diminishing function of increases in the rate of growth of output. It is well known that producers in their anxiety for security accumulate certain liquid reserves. These liquid reserves, when at an optimum level, can be expressed as a certain fraction of fixed assets, and since the ratio of fixed assets to output is here assumed constant, as a certain fraction of output.[1] Suppose now that this optimum ratio has been established and that it is desired to increase the rate of growth of output. Inevitably some of the liquid assets will get used up, the greater the rate of increase in output the greater will be the divergence from the optimum liquidity ratio. It is true that if the new rate of growth in output is maintained, liquidity can be built up to the optimum again. But during a certain period there will be too few liquid funds and therefore *ceteris paribus* uncertainty will be increased.[2] It is the change in the rate of growth in output which is responsible for this.

It does, therefore, seem fairly clear that uncertainty is an increasing function, and willingness to produce a diminishing function, of the increase in the rate of growth in output.[3] Moreover, as long as the rate of growth in output is increasing, production in general will be uncertain for the reasons already given. This implies that uncertainty will also increase with the absolute level of output, i.e. the absolute level of commitments. For in an uncertain world, i.e. a world where the rate of growth in output is changing, the greater one's commitments the greater the possible loss.

If the above analysis is correct then we shall expect, other things being equal, the share of wages to diminish in times when the rate of growth in output is increasing.

Since the uncertainty analysis refers to a situation where new commitments have to be undertaken, our above discussion does not apply *pari passu* to a negative rate of growth, for here there will be excess capacity and the whole situation will be changed. The case of a negative rate of growth will be discussed in a later chapter. What our analysis does show is that an increasing *positive* rate of growth will tend to increase the marginal uncertainty of production and, other things being equal, therefore reduce the share of wages. The full implication of this will be discussed more fully in subsequent chapters.

III

One drawback of the analysis so far is that it relies very heavily on an intuitive approach to entrepreneurial motivation and action. This in the present state of knowledge cannot be helped and we simply have to make do with conclusions qualified by such adjectives as 'probable' and 'likely' without being able to give any precise meaning to these qualifications. There is however a strong temptation to try and establish a theory by slightly less realistic, and more mechanical, but at the same time more precise, techniques.

This temptation is particularly strong when we try to compare dynamic with static equilibrium conditions. The former normally imply a constant rate of growth and we have already noted that this is unlikely in reality. Nevertheless certain valuable lessons may be gained from analysing the equilibrium conditions of this type. The rest of this chapter will be devoted to this analysis.

Hicks[4] has analysed a regular progressing economy under two assumptions: 1) when the only investment is induced investment and 2) when there is also autonomous investment growing at a certain constant rate g. He concluded from his analysis of these two systems that a progressing equilibrium is possible in case 1) whenever g (the equilibrium rate of growth) was positive and real and in case 2) when given g, the propensity to save at the equilibrium income was high enough to cover both autonomous and induced investment. But Hicks never explicitly examined the production side of the problem, i.e. he never sought to discover the conditions under which a given rate of growth of output can be provided at the optimum factor ratio. He therefore only gave the necessary but not the sufficient conditions for a progressing equilibrium. From our point of view this is of some importance. We shall therefore examine these additional conditions in some detail.

We shall postulate that all production functions are linear and homogeneous. We shall also (as does Hicks) assume there to be a production lag of one period. Making these assumptions ΔY_t, the increment in output which can be produced in period t at the optimum factor ratio is proportional to the investment I_{t-1} of period t – 1. We write

$$\Delta Y_t = \alpha I_{t-1}. \quad (6.1)$$

Assuming only induced investment (Hicks' case a]), and that the latter is lagged by one period we write

$$I_t = v(Y_{t-1} - Y_{t-2}) = v\Delta Y_{t-1}, \quad (6.2)$$

(where Y_{t-1}, Y_{t-2} are incomes of period t – 1 and t – 2 and v is the 'relation').
Substituting 6.2 into 6.1 we obtain

$$\Delta Y_t = \alpha v \Delta Y_{t-2}. \quad (6.3)$$

Now the solution of 6.3 contains two roots, $_1\lambda$ and $_2\lambda$ where $_1\lambda = +\sqrt{\alpha v}$ $(\alpha v > 0)$ and $_2\lambda = -\sqrt{\alpha v}$ and the solution is written as

$$\Delta Y_t = {}_1\lambda^t K_1 + {}_2\lambda^t K_2, \quad (6.4)$$

where K_1 and K_2 are derived from the initial conditions. If however we postulate that incomes have been growing at a constant rate over the past then $K_2 = 0$ and we may write 6.4 as

$$\Delta Y_t = {}_1\lambda^t K_1. \quad (6.5)$$

6.5 gives us the (constant) rate at which incomes will grow when the optimum factor ratio is preserved, i.e. when there is always sufficient investment to produce the required increase in output at the factor ratio which minimises costs.

The condition for a progressing equilibrium is now that the rate of growth in demand must equal the rate of growth in supply as given by 6.5 and that demand should equal supply. The latter assumption is always made by Hicks, but without distinguishing between a demand and supply equation.

Let us write Y^s_t as the *ex ante* supply of output in period t and Y^d_t as the *ex ante* demand for output in period t. Neglecting the possibility of decumulating stocks,[5] income in any period will equal Y^s_t. The demand for consumption C^d_t is assumed a function of yesterday's income Y^s_{t-1} and the demand for investment I^d_t in period t is a function of the rate of change in demand of the previous period. Therefore total demand Y^d_t in period t is given by

$$Y^d_t = cY^s_{t-1} + v(Y^d_{t-1} - Y^d_{t-2}), \quad (6.6)$$

(where c is the propensity to consume).
But for equilibrium we postulate $Y^s = Y^d$ throughout, so that we can drop the superscripts and write 6.6 as

$$Y_t = cY_{t-1} + v(Y_{t-1} - Y_{t-2}), \quad (6.7)$$

which is Hicks' output equation. But we must remember how we have arrived at 6.7, namely by postulating $Y^s = Y^d$. If this is to be valid for any period then demand must grow at the same rate as output. Let us put 6.7 into incremental form. We have

$$Y_t - Y_{t-1} = \Delta Y_t = c\Delta Y_{t-1} + v(\Delta Y_{t-1} - \Delta Y_{t-2}). \quad (6.8)$$

Our condition of progressing equilibrium now is that the solution of 6.8 should be the same as that of 6.3. The solution of 6.8 may be written as

$$Y_t = {}_1\gamma^t R_1 + {}_2\gamma^t R_2 \;({}_1\gamma \text{ and } {}_2\gamma \text{ both assumed real}), \quad (6.9)$$

where ${}_1\gamma$ and ${}_2\gamma$ are the roots of equation 6.8 and R_1 and R_2 are derived from the initial conditions. Once again if the rate of growth is constant $R_2 = 0$ and we have

$$Y_t = {}_1\gamma^t R_1. \quad (6.10)$$

Hence given that $Y^s = Y^d$ over the past, the condition for equilibrium is that ${}_1\lambda = {}_1\gamma$.

We shall examine the conditions which must be satisfied for the two roots to be equal. But before we do this we notice that the equilibrium rate of growth of output is intimately linked with the efficiency of investment (α) which nowhere appears in Hicks' analysis. In fact demand, if equilibrium is preserved, must not grow faster or more slowly than the growth in output made possible by past investment. This has important implications for the equilibrium distribution of income.

In particular we notice that the ratio of investment to output must always be such that any given rate of growth in output can be maintained at the optimum factor ratio. The higher the rate of growth in output the greater must be the proportion of income invested if this higher rate is to be produced at the optimum factor ratio throughout.[6] The question now arises: will the addition of an autonomous investment term to our equations make any difference (in kind) to the equilibrium conditions? Hicks believes that it does.

Now autonomous investment is nowhere precisely defined, and appears to be a convenient hold-all for any type of investment which is not induced by output changes. Frequently this type of investment is also regarded as due to innovations. This involves various difficulties, since on this view there would then be no good reason for regarding the induced investment coefficient v as constant. But we cannot enter into these difficulties in detail here. One thing however appears clear: a higher rate of growth of autonomous investment need not necessarily imply a higher rate of growth in productivity.

For the rate of growth of autonomous investment may change for a large number of reasons. For instance innovations may on balance become progressively more labour-saving and thus involve more investment per unit of output, without in any way raising the rate of growth in productivity. Again, if all sorts of other investment, not due to innovations but, say, to government or very long term investment, are included under autonomous investment, it is once again clear that there may be no direct relationship between the rate of growth in autonomous investment and the rate of growth in productivity.

If this is correct then our conclusions that a higher rate of growth in output implies a higher equilibrium ratio of investment to output may still be correct.

Let us suppose that there is a positive rate of population growth. It will then be possible for incomes to grow at a certain rate without innovations. Let us further assume that in fact no innovations are made but that there is nevertheless some autonomous investment. Now the fact that investment is autonomous does not mean that it contributes nothing to output. In fact on any economic definition of income all investment will be undertaken with a view to contributing to some future income. If this is true then we may write our equation 6.1 as follows:

$$\Delta Y_t = \alpha I_{t-1} + \beta H(1+g)^{t-1}, \quad (6.1a)$$

(where β is the production coefficient of autonomous investment H growing at a rate g, which is here assumed to contribute to output with a one period lag). From 6.1a it follows immediately that

$$g = \alpha \frac{I_{t-1}}{Y_{t-1}} + \frac{\beta H}{E}, \quad (6.1b)$$

where E is the equilibrium level of income.

It is clear once again that the equilibrium ratio of investment to output will increase with g as long as α and β are given and constant, even if autonomous investment is included. How do we account for the difference between Hicks' results and ours?

The answer I think lies in the fact that Hicks is greatly preoccupied with the Keynesian equilibrium conditions which are almost entirely framed in the form of aggregate demand and has neglected the equally important aspect of production equilibrium. Irrespective of the level of income, unless innovations are made which economise in the use of capital (i.e. raise α and/or β) a higher rate of growth of that income must involve a higher ratio of investment to output if income expansion is to proceed at the optimum factor ratio. For once a production lag is introduced, sufficient investment goods must be produced in any period t to provide for the planned increase in output in period t + 1. It is therefore only when future planned output is completely independent of autonomous investment in the past that it is possible to maintain any given ratio of investment to output by altering the level of income.

But surely a given rate of autonomous investment just as a given rate of induced investment makes a certain specific rate of growth in output possible at the optimum factor ratio. If that is so, then the equilibrium ratio of investment to output must increase with the equilibrium rate of growth, unless certain innovations are made. Consideration of these is postponed to a later chapter.

Enough has been said to show that unless the rate of growth in output that it is possible to maintain at the optimum factor ratio is independent of the rate of growth of autonomous investment, we are not at liberty to choose an equilibrium level of income which always keeps the ratio of investment to output constant no matter what the rate of growth of income.

Let us now return to the main argument. It can easily be shown[7] that if ${}_1\lambda = {}_1\gamma$, then

$$-v + \sqrt{\frac{(\alpha v + v)^2}{\alpha v}} = c. \quad (6.11)$$

Now we assume that the propensity to consume c is linearly related to $\frac{W}{Y}$ and write

$$c = z\frac{W}{Y} + k, \quad (6.12)$$

so that 6.11 becomes

$$\frac{1}{Z}\left[-v + \sqrt{\frac{(\alpha v + v)^2}{\alpha v}} - k\right] = \frac{W}{Y}. \quad (6.13)$$

6.13 gives us the equilibrium share of wages in terms of the efficiency of investment (α), the relation (v), and z. Now the larger z and k the larger is the propensity to consume of capitalists (non wage-earners) if we assume that wage-earners consume the whole of their income. The equilibrium share of wages is thus a diminishing function of z and k.

The higher v (the relation) the higher will generally be the rate of growth of income and hence the higher the equilibrium ratio of investment to income. Thus the lower will be the propensity to consume,[8] i.e. the lower will the share of wages have to be if $Y^s = Y^d$ throughout. The higher α (given v) the greater can the growth of income be without reducing $\frac{W}{Y}$.[9]

These then are the equilibrium conditions for the share of wages which we will attempt to interpret in the next section.[10] But it should be noticed here that our conclusions are remarkably close to some of the wage-fund theorists', and we shall examine this in the next chapter in greater detail. Here we are content to point out that our results are in accordance with common sense. The higher the rate of growth in income, the smaller is the proportion of income a community can consume, for a high rate of growth means a high rate of investment. Hence if a high rate of growth is established without people changing their consumption habits the share of wages must be reduced.

IV

These then are our 'mechanical' equilibrium conditions in a very simplified model. But it is evident that there is no guarantee that such an equilibrium will ever be reached. How then are we to interpret our results?

In the first place our analysis shows us what share of wages is *consistent,* given certain entrepreneurial decisions and the technical conditions of production, with an equilibrium between supply and demand through time. It does not tell us how this consistent share of wages is determined. Equilibrium, or maximum, conditions can never tell us that.

But we know already on general grounds that the share of wages in equilibrium will be such that producers have maximised their utility. Therefore to every technical coefficient of our equations (given factor prices and expectations) there will correspond certain entrepreneurial decision coefficients and therefore a certain share of wages for which these coefficients remain constant. But this share of wages may not be consistent with equilibrium as above defined. Thus, entrepreneurial decision coefficients – and the share of wages – will change again. There may thus (if we ignore the possibility of multiple equilibria) be one share of wages 1) for which producers have maximised their utility and their decision coefficients remain constant and 2) which is consistent with equilibrium as defined.

From our equations we find how the *consistent* share of wages will change when any of the coefficients change. From the production and entrepreneurial utility functions we could discover how the utility-maximising share of wages changes when any of the coefficients change. We therefore have enough information to determine the share of wages (if it exists) which is not only consistent with equilibrium between aggregate demand and supply but also maximises producers' utility at every moment of time. But we must repeat that in a dynamic analysis this equilibrium must always be treated as a point of reference only, for in practice it will not be attained.

Our analysis also reveals what seems to me frequently neglected, namely that if production takes time, equilibrium in our sense requires perfect foresight on the part of the entrepreneur. This makes this type of equilibrium doubly unlikely and in the next chapter this assumption will be dropped.

Since a regular progressing economy requires that there is perfect foresight the relation v in our equations is not determined as in Hicks' system. In the latter v is such that a given past increase in income is produced at the optimum factor ratio. Hicks' producers never expect demand to increase beyond yesterday's level. In our equations v is such that a given past increase in demand evokes sufficient investment to supply an expected future increase in demand at the optimum factor ratio. Our v thus is not purely dependent on the physical conditions of production but also on the expectations of producers as to future demand. I cannot see how this can be avoided if equilibrium is to be possible.

Lastly we may note that if the equilibrium share of wages is inversely related to the rate of growth in income, it will *a fortiori* also diminish with increases in the rate of growth. The results of our more intuitive approach are therefore confirmed.

Chapter 7

The wage fund theory reconsidered: a digression

In the previous chapter we reached the conclusion that the equilibrium share of wages would, given technological conditions of production, be a diminishing function of the equilibrium rate of growth and we noted that this conclusion bore a certain resemblance to the older doctrines of distribution based on the wage fund theory. It is the purpose of this chapter to examine this resemblance in greater detail.

I

Excellent surveys of the classical theory of distribution have been made by a number of eminent economists,[1] and it is therefore not proposed to describe either any particular theory or development of thought here. The salient features of most wage-fund doctrines may be outlined as follows:

1 Production takes time. Therefore the output of all goods in general and wage goods in particular available over a given period of time is determined by past decisions.

2 The total real wage of labour over this period of time cannot therefore exceed the total (predetermined) output of wage goods over the same period, assuming that wage earners spend all their income on wage goods.

3 Competition among labourers will ensure that everyone will be employed and the average real wage is therefore fully determined at any moment of time by the quantity of wage goods available and the number of labourers.

4 If there is continuous production and investment, the division of total income (output) between consumption goods and wage goods will be determined by the rate of interest and the wage rate, such that in equilibrium everyone is employed and profits are maximised.

5 Therefore from 1) to 4) it follows that the share of wages in the national income is equal to the ratio of wage goods to output, and this is determined (at least later 'neo-classicals' believed) by the relative productivities of labour and capital (roundaboutness) and by the total amount of labour available.

It is clear that this summary lumps together theories which were propounded fairly early on (e.g. by Adam Smith, Ricardo, McCulloch and Senior) with those which came later (e.g. Böhm Bawerk, Wicksell and Taussig). But we are not here concerned with discussing these theories in detail. We thus ignore such theories as were based on the assumption of a constant and fixed fund and we do not enter into the discussion which took place as to the factors determining the division of total capital into fixed and circulating. All these doctrines and assumptions were attacked by later wage-fund theorists and shown to be either incorrect or to tend to indeterminacy. In particular it must be remembered that the wage fund doctrine in its most precise statement does not preclude a marginal productivity theory of distribution, and really comes down to little more than the statement that wage earners could not, at any moment of time, consume more than was available, and that what was available for consumption depended on past decisions and the time it took to increase output (period of production).

But there is one assumption all wage fund theorists invariably made, namely that there would always be full employment. It is this assumption which has produced the cliché so frequently heard today that 'the classical theories apply when there is full employment, and Keynes' theories when there is unemployment'. But is this really so?

Full employment output is frequently defined as that level of output for which the supply curve becomes inelastic. Yet no one has seriously suggested that once full employment has been reached output will (if full employment is maintained) become stationary. As long as net investment continues output will grow through time. What is therefore meant by saying that classical theories of investment, savings etc., become applicable once full employment has been reached is presumably that output cannot be expanded immediately. But that is true for all levels of employment, although as long as there is excess capacity in equipment the production lag will be much shorter than when there is no such excess capacity.

There is therefore no difference in kind between the effect of an increase (or decrease) in demand when there is full employment and when there is unemployment, although there may be some differences in degree (e.g. the rate of interest may remain constant in the latter but not in the former case). Whatever the ultimate verdict on the difference between Keynesian and classical analysis may be, there is no doubt that the absence of the time dimension in most of Keynes' *General Theory* is one of the most important points of departure from classical writings where it played a conspicuous part.

At the same time the classical assumption of continuous full employment, while probably based on false theory, is a less serious obstacle to the analysis of a number of problems than is sometimes supposed. Clearly we would not now wish to accept their theory of employment as it stands, but as far as the theory of the share of wages is concerned that assumption (of full employment) is *not* necessary to the classical doctrine. For their main propositions would still hold if the money wage is fixed and given, provided we still retain the undoubtedly valid assumption that it takes time before an increase in output can be produced. For full employment need only be postulated if the wage of labour is to be determined.

II

With these preliminaries out of the way we may now attempt to fit the wage fund doctrine, in so far as it is relevant to the problem of distribution, into a more modern theory.

Given the money wage, and entrepreneurs' estimates of demand, each entrepreneur will employ, in any one period t, labour until its 'adjusted'[2] marginal value product is equal to its wage. This will then fully determine the total money wage bill in period t. Assuming that wage-earners spend the whole of their income in the current period on wage goods, and that capitalists' consumption of these is constant, wage-earners' real total wage in terms of wage goods will be determined by the total of wage goods available in the current period. For if prices are flexible, the total output of wage goods of period t will equal total real wages in that period. Therefore the total real wage of labour in period t cannot exceed the total of wage goods available in that period.

Equilibrium will therefore be achieved when the total money wage, as determined by employers' demand for labour at the given wage rate, is such that the demand for wage goods at the price ruling at the beginning of any period is equal to the amount of these supplied. And the share of wages will be in equilibrium (i.e. remain constant) when the ratio of wage goods to total output remains constant. If therefore output is growing then the output of wage goods must grow at the same rate as the output of all goods is growing.

We have already examined the implications of these conditions in the previous chapter. But we were not satisfied that these were very meaningful since it was unlikely that equilibrium, as defined there, would ever be reached. Moreover as far as the wage fund doctrine is concerned, whenever *ex ante* supply is equal to *ex ante* demand through time, it yields identical results to those of the present day theory of distribution. Equilibrium conditions are never very interesting, and the wage fund theories are most helpful in analysing how a particular equilibrium is reached rather than what the conditions of the latter are.

We shall therefore now drop the assumption of continuous equality between *ex ante* demand and *ex ante* supply, i.e. we shall no longer postulate perfect foresight. Instead we shall assume that the increase in output producers are willing to supply is a function of the excess demand of the previous period and that if the latter is zero, the increase in output will be zero. This assumption, while not entirely realistic, is more so than that of perfect foresight. Apart from that however it will help us to lay bare the essentials of the argument.

Let us now attempt to construct a dynamic model on the basis of this assumption. Using the notation of previous chapters, we may write as our first equation that the total real wage (W) in period t must equal the supply of wage goods.[3]

$$W_t = C^s_t. \quad (7.1)$$

Dividing both sides by Y_t we have

$$\frac{W_t}{Y_t} = \left(\frac{W}{Y}\right)_t = \frac{C^s_t}{Y_t} = c^s_t. \quad (7.2)$$

Equation 7.2 tells us that the share of wages in period t must equal the proportion of output which is in the form of wage goods (c^s_t).

But the supply of wage goods in period t will have been determined by past decisions and these will have been based on past demand and supply conditions. We write our supply equation of wage goods as follows:

$$C^s_t = C^s_{t-1} + m(C^d_{t-1} - C^s_{t-1}), \quad (7.3)$$

that is to say we assume that producers will supply an amount of wage goods in period t equal to what they produced in period t−1 plus an amount proportional to the excess demand of that period.

Putting 7.3 into terms of proportion of total income supplied in wage goods we have

$$c^s_t Y_t = c^s_{t-1} Y_{t-1} + m\,(c^d_{t-1} Y_{t-1} - c^s_{t-1} Y_{t-1}), \quad (7.4)$$

where c^d_{t-1} is the proportion of yesterday's income demanded in the form of consumption goods. Putting $\frac{Y_{t-1}}{Y_t} = \mu$ = constant, and dividing 7.4 through by Y_t we have

$$c^s_t = c^s_{t-1}\,\mu + m\mu\,(c^d_{t-1} - c^s_{t-1}). \quad (7.5)$$

Now, we know from our previous discussion that if the demand for wage goods exceeds their supply that the share of wages will fall below the level at which producers have maximised their utility. This is only another way of saying that prices (of wage goods) will rise in period t above the level at which they were fixed at the beginning of the period (i.e. profits will rise). If we denote by $\left(\frac{W}{Y}\right)_e$ the share of wages at which producers have maximised their utility, and assume it constant, then the proportion of output demanded in the form of wage goods at the beginning of the period will be equal to this 'equilibrium' share of wages. We may therefore write

$$c^d_t = \left(\frac{W}{Y}\right)_e = \text{constant.} \quad (7.6)$$

Using 7.6 and substituting 7.5 in 7.2 we have

$$\left(\frac{W}{Y}\right)_t = \mu\left(\frac{W}{Y}\right)_{t-1} + m\mu\left[\left(\frac{W}{Y}\right)_e - \left(\frac{W}{Y}\right)_{t-1}\right]. \quad (7.7)$$

From 7.7 we find immediately that if $\left(\frac{W}{Y}\right)$ is constant at $\left(\frac{\overline{W}}{Y}\right)$ it will be given by the equation

$$\left(\frac{\overline{W}}{Y}\right) = \frac{m\mu\left(\frac{W}{Y}\right)_e}{1 - \mu + m\mu}. \quad (7.8)$$

Hence if $\mu = 1$, i.e. the level of income remains constant, then if the share of wages also remains constant, it will equal the share which also maximises producers' profits. If $\mu < 1$, i.e. incomes are rising, then if the share of wages is constant it will be less than the share which maximises producers' profits. If $\mu > 1$, i.e. incomes are falling, then $\left(\frac{\overline{W}}{Y}\right) > \left(\frac{W}{Y}\right)_e$. This follows at once from our assumptions a) that the output of wage goods will only increase if there is excess demand and b) that it takes one period before an increased output can be produced. Hence if incomes are rising, this implies continued excess demand and this in turn implies that the share of wages will be less than its equilibrium value.

We now see that our assumptions lead us to the conclusion that the equilibrium rate of growth must be zero. This is clearly a special case, for it is possible that producers increase output even when there is no excess demand but in anticipation of rising demand. We could easily alter our model to take account of this, e.g. by postulating that supply in period t, in addition to being proportional to the excess demand of the previous period, is also proportional to the rate of growth of demand in that period.[4] We could then find that value of μ, say μ_0 (< 1) for which $\left(\frac{\overline{W}}{Y}\right) = \left(\frac{W}{Y}\right)_e$. But μ is here exogenously given (see post). Hence if $\mu < \mu_0$, $\left(\frac{\overline{W}}{Y}\right) < \left(\frac{W}{Y}\right)_e$ and vice versa for $\mu > \mu_0$. But if $\mu = \mu_0$ then that must imply that there is no excess demand (positive or negative), i.e. that *ex ante* supply is always equal to *ex ante* demand. That is very unlikely in the real world, hence normally we shall expect $\mu \neq 1$ or μ_0, and therefore $\left(\frac{W}{Y}\right)_e \neq \left(\frac{W}{Y}\right)_t$. Hence to assume that $\mu_0 = 1$, as we have done in the model above, simplifies analysis without affecting our general conclusions.

Equation 7.7 in our model has a solution consisting of a constant part (7.8) and a transient part given by

$$\left(\frac{w}{y}\right)_t = \left(\frac{w}{y}\right)_{t-1} (\mu - m\mu)^t, \quad (7.9)$$

where $\left(\frac{w}{y}\right)_t$ is the difference between the actual share of wages at any moment of time and the constant $\left(\frac{\overline{W}}{Y}\right)$. Once again, if $\mu = 1$, i.e. incomes are constant, then this implies that producers expect demand to remain constant, hence m = 1 and hence 7.9 is equal to zero. If $\mu < 1$, incomes increasing, then m will probably be greater than one, so that $(\mu - m\mu) < 0$ and thus the transient part will oscillate. As long as m is not very large however these oscillations will be damped.

Up to now however we have assumed μ to be given and this clearly is not a legitimate assumption to make since the action of producers of consumers' goods will affect the rate of growth of total income. Let us see how this difficulty can be overcome.

Total output at period t is equal to the sum of wage and investment goods produced. Suppose now that at the beginning of the period the demand for investment goods is equal to their supply but that there is excess demand for consumption goods. Assuming there to be no reaction lag (and no excess capacity) producers of these goods will now increase their investment demand. Therefore in the next period the output of both consumption and investment goods will increase. If now the output of wage goods and investment goods increase in the same proportion, then, assuming constant returns, employment will also increase in that proportion and therefore, given the money wage of labour, the excess demand for wage goods will continue in period t + 1. It is therefore quite possible for the excess demand for wage goods to be continuous. Moreover, as long as both producers of investment and wage goods behave in a similar fashion, i.e. only increasing output in response to excess demand, and as long as we continue to assume a one period lag only, the rate of growth in output can remain constant so long as producers' 'reaction coefficients' remain constant.

This of course does not mean that the rate of growth in output will in fact remain constant, since normally we shall have to take account of distributed lags, and, in any case, there is no reason why producers' reaction coefficients should remain constant. It is therefore possible that the rate of growth will be changing and approaching its equilibrium value. But in this chapter we are not concerned with the equilibrium distribution. It is therefore quite sufficient to have shown that it is possible for disequilibrium to be permanent, i.e. that μ can remain permanently above or below μ_0, or can even move further away from it. The existence of the trade cycle testifies to the fact that this can in fact happen.

III

How far then have we 'rehabilitated' the wage fund theory? Clearly not at all as far as the theory of employment is concerned, for we have postulated fixed money wages and unemployment. Clearly not as far as the classical doctrine of the rate of interest is concerned, for the latter plays no part in our analysis. We are thus left with the classical proposition that the share of wages will equal the ratio of wage goods to total output. No modern theorist nurtured on the *General Theory* and the modern theory of distribution will object to this conclusion.

Yet it is by no means trivial. For if there is not complete equilibrium, i.e. *ex ante* demand not equal to *ex ante* supply, the modern theory is not very helpful, while the classical is. There is nothing in the wage fund doctrine which precludes the use of marginal productivity and profit (or utility) maximisation as factors determining the share of wages. Indeed, our $\left(\frac{W}{Y}\right)_e$ is derived from these categories. But as we have shown it is only in special circumstances that $\left(\frac{W}{Y}\right) = \left(\frac{W}{Y}\right)_e$ and it is therefore only then that the present day theory gives us the correct answer to what the share of wages is at any one moment of time. The classical theory however, with its insistence on the time element in production, provides us with a tool whereby the share of wages can be determined, even when the economy is not in equilibrium.

It is true that the wage fund theories are themselves equilibrium theories, but this is due to the fact that they used the fund not only to determine the share of wages but also the level of wages. There is no reason why this should be done today. For however wrong the classical theorists may have been about the theory of employment, this certainly was not their only contribution to economic theory. It is their realisation that supply cannot be increased instantaneously (a fact frequently forgotten today, e.g. in the theory of the multiplier) which makes their theory of distribution as valuable today as it was fifty years ago. It matters little for our purposes that they made use of average periods of production which, on closer inspection, could not be defined, or that they (but by no means all) had no proper theory of the demand for a factor by a firm or industry. The fact remains that theirs is the only attempt to construct a macro-economic and dynamic theory of distribution.

In our model we made assumptions which, with the exception of continuous full employment, corresponded closely to those made by the wage fund theorists. We assumed that supply today was determined by demand yesterday, i.e. that production takes time and that the total real wage in any one period was equal to the output of wage goods of that period (i.e. we assumed flexible prices). But we also made use of the orthodox assumption that there will be one share of wages at which producers have maximised their profits (utility), i.e. at which wages are equal to the adjusted marginal product of labour. None of these assumptions is in any way drastic, except perhaps that of flexible prices. But they lead to results where orthodox theory does not.

We are far too apt today to regard income as the main variable of the system which brings it into equilibrium. Prices and the rate of interest –

those classical equilibrating factors – are fixed in rigid immobility, and incomes move up or down in response to the slightest disturbance. But once production and other lags are introduced there is no reason why income fluctuations should be capable of performing their equilibrating task – in fact, there is no reason, and all appearances seem to support the conclusion, why equilibrium should ever be attained. This being the case, it is neither correct nor very interesting to analyse the problem of distribution on the assumption that the individual firms of the system are always in equilibrium nor is it justifiable, whatever the shape of the cost function, to assume all prices constant and fixed.

Moreover, the Marshallian belief that in the 'long run' everything would come right and equilibrium be restored has little meaning in a world of lagged reactions and when production takes time. The wage fund approach has the advantage of enabling us to determine the present share of wages without having to wait for a hypothetical long run equilibrium to materialise. But not only that, it also aids us in deciding whether such a long run equilibrium can be achieved and in what circumstances and under what conditions. It therefore seems to me in all senses superior to the present approach, for in equilibrium it yields the same results as the latter and out of equilibrium it provides us with answers where the latter cannot.

We may sum up our conclusions as follows:

1 The wage fund theory (in its most developed form) of distribution can not only take account of the modern equilibrium determinants of the distribution of income (e.g. marginal productivity) but can also help us to determine the share of wages when there is not equilibrium.

2 There is no *a priori* reason why equilibrium should ever be attained, but if it is the wage fund theory yields identical results to the modern marginal productivity theory.

3 The most important contribution classical theory can make to modern analysis is its recognition of the time dimension in the production process. When the latter is incorporated into current day dynamic analysis we can get a determinate system of distribution without either postulating full employment or equilibrium.

4 We have found that just as in the short run, and neglecting lags, there corresponds one equilibrium level of income to every value of the share of wages, so when time lags are taken into account there corresponds one equilibrium rate of growth of income to every value of the share of wages. In the classical model the greater investment, the lower would be the real wage at any one moment of time. But the classicals failed to provide a theory of the rate of growth of output and of the wage fund. Their analysis

was therefore found deficient by modern theorists. In our model however such a theory is provided and we were thus able to extend the classical argument to deal with a growing wage fund. We found that the greater the rate of growth of output the greater would be the ratio of investment to current output, and therefore the lower the equilibrium share of wages. Since in the classical model the possible rate of growth of output was a function of t the period of production, and since the higher the latter the lower the share of wages, they reached similar results to ours although by a route we would not now be prepared to travel.

It is evident from this summary of our results that the comparison between our model and the wage fund theory cannot be pushed too far, even though there are many points of contact between them.

The time has now come for us to examine certain specific dynamic situations. Up to now we have said very little about what the actual rate of growth of output would be. This question is closely linked with the problem of the trade cycle and we must therefore turn our attention to the latter and its effects on the share of wages.

Chapter 8

The share of wages in the trade cycle: I

The previous two chapters have been concerned with examining certain general problems which arise in a dynamic theory of distribution. We argued there that the possibilities of dynamic equilibrium (at least for any length of time) were remote in the real world. A dynamic theory of distribution must therefore inevitably be examined within the framework of the trade cycle. It is accordingly the purpose of this and the following chapter to analyse the movements in the share of wages (if any) which occur during the course of the cycle.

This analysis must be conducted on two fronts. In the first place we must provide a theory of the behaviour of individual units of decision (firms etc.) during the course of the cycle. In the second place we must fit this micro-economic theory into a general macro-economic framework. Unfortunately this separation of tasks cannot be carried very far in a dynamic analysis since then *ex hypothesi* the various schedules etc. facing individual units of decision are shifting, i.e. we cannot assume 'other things' to be equal. Nevertheless it will be convenient to keep these two lines of approach separate.

This chapter will therefore be mainly devoted to the analysis of the distribution of income within an individual firm (or industry) over the course of the cycle, while the next chapter is an attempt to present a macro-economic theory.

I

Most economists when examining the behaviour of an individual firm during the course of the trade cycle assume that entrepreneurs equate marginal cost to marginal revenue for every level of output and at every moment of time. From this assumption older theorists argued that real wages would fall during the upswing, while more recent writings on this topic based on the same assumption seem to indicate that real wages can either fall or rise during the upward phase and that no *a priori* judgment is possible. Let us examine these in some greater detail.

The view that real wages would fall during the upswing was founded on the model of perfect competition. Stability of perfect competition prices demands that at the equilibrium output marginal costs should be rising. Money wages being assumed constant, this implied that the marginal product of labour would fall whenever increases in output occurred.

This explanation however is only correct under certain further assumptions which are not specifically stated. The perfect competition model *par excellence* assumes that entrepreneurs are homogeneous and that they use homogeneous factors in perfectly elastic supply to the individual firm. From this it follows that, in the absence of external economies, the supply curve of the industry (Marshall's particular expenses curve) will be horizontal. If this is so, when the demand curve of the industry shifts to the right, and when equilibrium *both* of the firms and the industry have been re-established, prices will have remained constant at their old level, and the whole of the increased output will have been supplied by the entry of new firms and none by the expansion of existing firms. That is to say, the above mentioned conclusions are only valid as long as the industry is in disequilibrium.

Hence the fall in real wages, which occurs during the upswing, when perfect competition is assumed, is due to a lag between an increase in demand (and super-normal profits) and the entry of new firms. It is this lag which is at least as much responsible for the fall in real wages as are the stability conditions of equilibrium. Since we would all agree that such a lag exists, it is reasonable to conclude that under perfect competition real wages will fall.

But modern economists almost automatically suspect conclusions based on the model world of perfect competition. Let us therefore extend our analysis to cover different market forms.

It is well known that stable equilibrium under monopolistic competition is perfectly compatible with diminishing marginal costs, provided they diminish less rapidly than marginal revenue. Hence if we assume sticky money wages when demand is expanding, prices may well fall and real wages rise. Again, if the supply curve of labour to the firm is less than perfectly elastic, then stable equilibrium in the labour market is perfectly compatible with increasing marginal productivity, provided it increases less rapidly than the marginal wage of labour. In general it can be shown that the whole economic system can be in stable equilibrium, provided total output increases more rapidly than the marginal revenue product of the factors of production including labour.[1]

But are we really satisfied with this analysis? Two problems seem to have remained unexamined.

1 Why should firms invest when they have (large) excess capacity? And if they do invest why should they be on their long run cost curves in the upswing?

2 Given the lag between the earning of super-normal profits and the entry of new firms, why should firms be on the downward sloping part of their average (long run) cost curve except at the beginning of the upturn?

The question asked in 1) we have already met with when discussing Kalecki's theory of distribution. We found there great difficulty in seeing how all supernormal profits could be competed away if there are large indivisibilities which seem to be implied by excess capacity. If however the cost curve is downward sloping, as has recently been maintained simply because there are economies of scale and not because of excess capacity in the old sense, then this difficulty disappears.

But another one takes its place. Ever since Marshall's *Principles* appeared, economists have distinguished between short and long run cost curves, and have maintained that the former is relevant when only a few of the factors (mainly labour and raw materials) are variable. Now, as we hope to show in the next chapter, it is highly probable that in the course of an upswing producers will find that they cannot get sufficient capital to produce each output at the optimum (minimum long run cost) factor ratio. For during the upswing demand is continuously increasing and given that it takes time to invest (which, after all, is Marshall's main reason for distinguishing between short and long run) and that it takes time for producers to react to an increase in demand, they will find themselves operating on their short and *not* on their long run cost curves.

If this is correct then the situation has changed materially. For the long run curve is the envelope of a large number of short run cost curves, and therefore short run marginal costs are rising above long run marginal costs at the point of tangency of the long run and short run average cost curves. Hence if the elasticity of demand is unchanged and wages are constant, prices will rise and real wages fall.

But it may now be argued that there may in fact be excess capacity throughout the greater part of the upswing, although it is difficult to see why the latter should then be characterised by increased investment.[2] This leads us to the second question we asked. Suppose for a moment that there is excess capacity and that the average cost curve is tangential to the (downward sloping) demand curve. Demand now increases and firms expand output and earn supernormal profits. Why should the increase in demand throughout the upswing be always such that the marginal revenue curve cuts the marginal cost curve at a point where the latter is falling? If this is so for every firm, and if there is excess capacity everywhere throughout, the stock of capital would never rise! This is surely absurd. At best therefore we can admit that during the early stages of the boom when there is still considerable excess capacity, real wages may rise but they will certainly fall once excess capacity has been exhausted.

The truth of the matter is that stability conditions of the type here discussed are wholly inappropriate for an analysis of the effect of large changes such as are involved in the trade cycle on the output and price policy of an individual firm. After all, these stability conditions are expressed in the language of the differential calculus which deals with infinitely small change, and in any case take no explicit account of the time element of adjustment. Not very great reliance can therefore be placed on the results of the analysis in which they are used.

So far we have concluded that, both under perfect and monopolistic competition, real wages are likely to fall in the upswing. But what of oligopoly?

In the case of oligopoly the use of stability conditions breaks down altogether. For here stability must refer to the maintenance or non-maintenance of group discipline when one of the parameters changes. The shape of the cost curves can give us little aid in determining how the real reward of labour will change when demand is increasing. On the other hand, as was mentioned elsewhere, the existence of price leadership provides us with a means of predicting probable changes. If the price leader's marginal costs are rising, the prices charged by the group as a whole are likely to rise. Moreover, it is well known that in times of rising and rapidly changing demand, group discipline will tend to break down or in any case be weakened, so that the group as a whole is likely to behave in a similar fashion to an ordinary producer faced with a continuous demand curve. If then our analysis is correct and most producers find that they are forced to produce on the short run cost curves, real wages will also tend to fall when there is oligopoly.

Up to now however we have simply spoken of shifts in the demand schedules facing producers and have said little about possible changes in their slope. Further, we have also continued to assume that producers will always charge a price and produce an output such that their marginal costs are equal to their marginal revenue throughout. These assumptions must now be examined.

One notable attempt to assess the change in the form of the relevant functions in times of expansion and contraction is due to Harrod.[3] In a well known proposition he maintains that owing to more careful buying in times of depression, and less careful buying in times of booms, the elasticity of demand will be higher in the former situation than in the latter. From this he then deduces the theorem, that real wages $F'(L)\,(1 - \frac{1}{e})$ (where $F'(L)$ is the marginal product of labour and e the elasticity of demand) will be higher in the depression than in the boom. But as has been pointed out by Robinson,[4] the reverse influence is exerted on the elasticity of demand by increased cartelisation in times of depression and by diminished cartelisation in times of booms, and therefore not too much reliance can be placed on Harrod's theory.

Let us now turn to the second assumption, that marginal costs are always equal to marginal revenue. In the first place it should be noted that a producer equates expected marginal cost to expected marginal revenue and that the actual values of these quantities may be different from their expected values. Secondly, the price producers charge and the output they produce today will be greatly influenced by what they expect to happen tomorrow or the day after tomorrow. It is thus conceivable that though short run marginal costs are rising, producers continue to base their price policy on expected long run marginal costs. If this is so then the real wage of labour may diverge indefinitely from its marginal product.

In recent times such criticisms of the marginal analysis of the firm have been voiced by a growing number of economists. While no doubt there is some substance in these, one feels that their point of view can be greatly exaggerated. It is true that the economic horizon of ordinary entrepreneurs extends over more than just one period. It is true that entrepreneurs have no clear conception of either marginal costs or marginal revenues. It is therefore also true that when economists use the marginal model to analyse the effects of very small changes in any parameter on the behaviour of the firm their margin of error is likely to be large. But when the changes themselves are discrete and large, this margin of error is likely to be far smaller. Thus if short run costs are rising steeply, it is highly improbable that entrepreneurs will reduce their price because, say, long run marginal costs are falling, and it is more than likely that they will in fact raise their price. In a similar way a small change in the rate of interest (say of the order of a half to one and a half percent) may have little effect on investment demand but a change of, say, five to ten percent almost certainly will. In a cycle changes tend to be large compared with a given equilibrium and the orthodox analysis will tend to give a correct answer, at least as far as the direction of the change is concerned.

But we have, earlier in this book, laid some stress on the utility function of the entrepreneur and on its importance in the analysis of the firm. Using the assumptions we made there, we found that an increasing rate of growth of output would tend to be associated with a rising marginal disutility of production. Now during the upswing the rate of growth is increasing (at least for a certain time) and hence we shall expect marginal profits to increase. Put differently, we shall expect the 'exploitation coefficient' to increase even if the elasticity of demand remains constant throughout.

In a depression entrepreneurs, because they have unwanted excess capacity, equate marginal gross profit to the marginal disutility of production. In the upswing, when excess capacity has been exhausted, it will be marginal net profit which will equal the marginal disutility of production. Unless we postulate a drastic change in the utility functions of the entrepreneurs caused by the greater optimism engendered by the boom, this factor alone will be sufficient to cause a fall in real wages. If, assuming for the moment constant costs and constant elasticities of demand, real wages were actually to rise, the marginal disutility of production would have to fall considerably. Given the 'depression consciousness' of modern entrepreneurs and their pre-occupation with security, this seems extremely unlikely, although of course we cannot be certain.

The conclusions of this section may be summarised as follows: in so far as the boom is associated with increased investment, most firms will have little or no excess capacity, except perhaps in the early stages of the boom. Since demand is continuously increasing and since investment decisions take time to be made and investment orders take time to be filled, most firms will be continually operating on their short run and not their long run cost curves. Since the latter are rising, real wages will fall. An increase in the elasticity of demand or a (considerable) fall in the marginal disutility of producing (owing to a change in the utility function of entrepreneurs) may be sufficient to offset this tendency, but this seems unlikely. The above conclusions will apply whether there is perfect competition, monopolistic competition or oligopoly.

II

A similar analysis can be applied to the downturn. Now demand is continuously falling. Firms will find that they have a great deal of excess capacity. Producers will be willing to produce as long as total revenue exceeds total prime costs by a very small margin (equal to the marginal disutility of production). Because of all these factors, the marginal product of labour will tend to rise.

For in the depression the marginal cost of using capital will be zero or near zero. Hence from the point of view of the entrepreneur the optimum factor combination will be the one for which the marginal product of capital is zero or near zero. This change in the factor ratio can be accomplished without any great lag, and once accomplished can be maintained. In so far therefore as the coefficients of production are variable, there will be a sharp change in the factor ratio between boom and slump. This will be decisive in raising the marginal product of labour and therefore its real wage.

It may now be objected that since in a depression oligopolistic forces tend to be particularly strong, entrepreneurs will in fact not equate the wage of labour to its (adjusted) marginal product. But I don't think that this objection is serious. It is precisely because entrepreneurs in the initial stages of the downswing attempt to reach their most profitable position independently of others, i.e. because they lower prices, that a spur is given to collective producers' action. But once the cartel or any producers' association is formed it is extremely unlikely that they will do more than stabilise prices and almost certainly will not raise them. The formation of oligopolistic groups in the depression therefore may prevent real wages from rising by as much as they would otherwise have done, but it is highly unlikely that they will prevent the rise altogether.

Since producers are now equating their marginal disutility of production to the marginal gross and not the marginal net profit, this will tend to reduce the 'exploitation coefficient' and to raise real wages. It is of course possible that their utility functions will change in such a manner as to raise their marginal disutility of production above its boom value. But this is highly unlikely. In a depression one of the prime needs of producers is greater liquidity to meet commitments undertaken in the boom. The only way such liquidity can be achieved is by producing as long as gross profits are not negative (and perhaps even then to prevent bankruptcy). On the whole therefore we would expect the disutility factor to work in the direction of raising real wages.

Lastly, it is possible that the elasticity of demand will fall. We have however decided to maintain an agnostic attitude to this possibility. We can therefore do no more than acknowledge that this is a possibility, and that if it occurs real wages will not rise by as much as they would otherwise have done or may even fall.

On the whole however the arguments seem overwhelmingly to suggest a rise in real wages in the depression.

III

We have now finished our discussion of changes in real wages during the course of the trade cycle. But we have assumed that money wages and raw material prices remain constant throughout. We have also defined real wages in terms of labour's own product and not in terms of wage goods. Both the assumptions and definition will be re-examined in the next section. In this section however we wish to take the step from an analysis of real wages to that of the share of wages when all these assumptions are still made.

Let us first examine the boom. We have argued that during this phase of the cycle most producers will be operating on their short run cost curves. We now further assume that they always equate marginal short run cost with marginal revenue (see post).

Let us write K for total cost, L for the amount of labour employed, P^L for the (constant) price of labour, C for the quantity of capital and P^c for the (constant) price of capital. We assume that the ratio of raw material costs to wage costs remains constant throughout, so that we ignore the former for the moment. We have

$$K = P^L L + P^c C, \quad (8.1)$$

and short run marginal cost is given by

$$\frac{dK}{dx} = P^L \frac{dL}{dx} \quad (C = \text{constant}). \quad (8.2)$$

By a well known formula we may write marginal revenue equal to $P(1 - \frac{1}{e})$, where P = price of output, e = elasticity of demand. We have for short run equilibrium

$$P(1 - \frac{1}{e}) = P^L \frac{dL}{dx}. \quad (8.3)$$

Multiplying P^L by $\frac{L}{x}$ and dividing $\frac{dL}{dx}$ by $\frac{L}{x}$, and dividing 8.3 by P we have

$$\left(1 - \frac{1}{e}\right) = \frac{P^L L}{xP} \frac{dL}{dx} \frac{x}{L} \quad (8.4)$$

Now $\frac{P^L L}{xP}$ is the share of wages in our firm at any one moment of time which we shall write as $\left(\frac{W}{R}\right)$, and $\frac{dL}{dx}\frac{x}{L}$ may be defined as the output elasticity of demand for labour which we write as ϵ. W is the total money wage bill and R is total revenue. Rearranging 8.4 we have

$$\frac{\left(1 - \frac{1}{e}\right)}{\epsilon} = \frac{W}{R}. \quad (8.5)$$

It follows from 8.5 that as long as e and ϵ are constant the share of wages will remain constant.

Now in the depression there was (unwanted) excess capacity, so that we can assume that producers equated marginal short run (prime) cost to marginal revenue. If now in the boom they find that they have insufficient capital, they will once again be operating on their short run cost curves. But in the depression prime costs will have been constant or falling, that is $\epsilon \leqslant 1$. If then marginal short run costs in the boom are rising, i.e. $\epsilon > 1$, then given e, the share of wages must be lower in the boom than in the depression (by 8.5).

Let us next assume that producers are on their long run cost curves in the depression but that in the course of the expansion they are forced on to their short run cost curves owing to a shortage of capital. Let us also assume that both average and long run costs are falling. Now long run marginal cost is given by

$$\frac{dK}{dx} = P^L \frac{dL}{dx} + P^c \frac{dC}{dx}, \quad (8.6)$$

from which we easily find

$$\frac{\left(1 - \frac{1}{e}\right) - P^c \frac{dc}{dx}}{\epsilon} = \frac{W}{R}. \quad (8.7)$$

If now output is increased, but the quantity of capital and the elasticity of demand remain constant we find that

$$\frac{d}{dx}\left(\frac{W}{R}\right) = \frac{d}{dx}\left(\frac{\left(1-\frac{1}{e}\right)-P^c\frac{dC}{dx}}{\epsilon}\right) = -\frac{\left[\left(1-\frac{1}{e}\right)-P^c\frac{dC}{dx}\right]}{\epsilon^2}\frac{d\epsilon}{dx}. \quad (8.8)$$

Hence $\frac{d}{dx}\left(\frac{W}{R}\right)$ is $>$ or <0 according as $\frac{d\epsilon}{dx}$ is $<$ or $>$ 0. Since we have assumed that the short run marginal cost curve is falling it is possible that $\frac{d\epsilon}{dx} < 0$ and hence that the share of wages will increase.

But we must remember that in the upswing demand will be increasing continually and that it is very probable that it will be increasing at an increasing rate for at least part of the boom. This will be discussed more fully in the next chapter. Here however we may note that if demand is increasing at an increasing rate (demand curves shifting to the right at an increasing rate) and if it always takes one period to instal more capital and if producers always instal sufficient in any one period to produce last period's output at minimum cost, then the ratio of the optimum stock of capital to the desired stock of capital will also be increasing. It therefore seems unrealistic to assume falling short run marginal costs for any great part of the expansion. So that even if the share of wages increases initially it will sooner or later diminish again and go on diminishing as increasing marginal costs are encountered.

Assuming all factor prices constant and the elasticity of demand unchanged, we may now classify the following results:

1 If at no time producers are able to produce at the optimum factor ratio, and if the boom short run marginal cost curve is rising while the slump short run marginal cost curve is constant, the share of wages will be less in the boom than in the depression.

2 If in the depression producers are on their long run marginal cost curves and the latter are constant (constant returns to scale, $\epsilon = 1$) and if during the boom they are forced on to their short run marginal cost curves, then since the latter must be rising, $\epsilon > 1$ and the boom share of wages will again be below the slump share.

3 If the long run marginal cost curve on which producers are operating in the depression is falling, and if in the expansion producers are forced on to their (falling) short run marginal cost curves, then it is possible that the boom share of wages may be higher than the depression share. But it is unlikely that short run marginal costs will be falling for any significant part

of the expansion.

Partial analysis will not carry us much further than this. For we need a general theory of the cycle before we can decide whether producers will on the average be forced to produce on their short run cost curves during the upswing or not. This problem will be examined in some detail in the next chapter. But in so far as there is any validity in the distinction between long run and short run cost curves, we can take it almost for granted that short run and not long run cost curves will be relevant in the boom.

We must however not forget the assumptions we have been making. We have assumed that all factor prices will remain constant, that the elasticity of demand is unchanged and that there are no innovations. None of these assumptions is likely to be fulfilled and the analysis of this chapter must therefore be regarded as a first approach only. Innovations we shall discuss in a later chapter, but we cannot postpone a discussion of changing money wages any further.

IV

We must now relax the assumption of constant money wages and zero raw material prices.

Most economists, at least until recently, have believed that during a boom money wages would lag behind prices. Thus Marshall maintained that

> 'where prices are rising, the rise in the price of the finished commodity is generally more rapid than that in the price of labour, and when prices are falling the fall in the price of the finished commodity is generally more rapid than that in the price of raw materials and always more rapid than in the price of labour.'[5]

This assumption was also made by Keynes when he hazarded the guess that real wages could be falling when money wages are rising.

A number of statistical investigations into this problem were made[6] and it was found by at least one writer that real wages frequently rose when money wages were rising. But in this investigation the real wage of labour was defined in terms of wage goods and that clearly is inadmissible in testing the validity of a theory in which real wages are defined in terms of labour's own product. A recent investigation into the subject, using the correct definition of real wages, concludes that

> 'Rises in the average money wage rates were more often associated with

decreases than with increases in product wage rates measured in this way, both in the United States and Great Britain. And falls in the average money wage rates were more often associated with increases rather than with decreases in product wage rates in the system as a whole. But there were a number of instances where a sharp change in money wages brought about a change in product wages in the same direction.'[7]

The evidence therefore seems to favour Keynes' hunch on this matter. For a thorough-going theoretical discussion we would need a theory of trade union behaviour, and although a number of such theories exist they are on the whole unconvincing and in any case give us little help in answering the question of whether money wages lag behind prices. We must therefore continue to regard money wage movements as exogenously determined.

Let us first assume that each producer is faced with an upward rising supply curve of labour but that the supply curve does not shift. Then the marginal prime cost (still excluding raw materials) becomes

$$P^L \frac{dL}{dx} + L\frac{dP^L}{dx}, \quad (8.9)$$

from which we find that in equilibrium

$$\frac{\left(1 - \frac{1}{e}\right)}{\epsilon + \eta} = \frac{W}{R}, \quad (8.10)$$

where $\eta = \frac{dP^L}{dx} \cdot \frac{x}{P^L}$ the output elasticity of wages. It is clear from 8.10 that the higher η the lower $\frac{W}{R}$ and therefore *ceteris paribus* the lower the real wage of labour. Thus if money wages rise as output increases without there being a shift in the supply curve, the share of wages will fall.

But normally when speaking of a rise in money wages during the boom, we have in mind an upward shift in the supply curve of labour facing each producer. This means that the marginal cost curves of figure 8, chapter 9 will be raised without necessarily affecting their slope. It is now time that we took account of the raw material component in prime costs.

If money wages rise without affecting the price of raw materials then the prime cost curve will rise less than in proportion to the rise in money wages. Thus even if, as is assumed by Lange,[8] all the demand curves are shifted to the right, such that at the new intersection of marginal short run cost and marginal revenue the slopes of average short run cost and average revenue are the same as before, the share of wages will rise since total wages now constitute a higher proportion of prime costs. We can therefore safely conclude that if money wages rise relatively to raw material prices, the ratio between raw materials and labour being given, the share of wages (and real wages) will either increase or fall by less than they would otherwise have done. Hence rising money wages will be favourable to the share of wages whenever they rise relatively to the prices of raw materials.

But it must be remembered that raw material prices tend to rise relatively to money wages in an expansion. This has recently been confirmed beyond doubt by Tsiang.[9] This is probably due to the fact that the short run supply curve of raw materials tends to be rather inelastic. If this is so then rising money wages will not be able to prevent either the fall in real wages or in the share of wages. But on the other hand any rise in money wages, in the sense of an upward shift in the supply curve of labour, will prevent the share of wages from falling by as much as it would have done if money wages had remained constant.

If we introduce lags into the analysis it rapidly becomes very complicated, because not only will the cost curve be shifting but so also will the demand curve. It is conceivable that wages do not lag behind prices, but the latter lag behind wages, and then rising money wages would most probably be associated with rising real wages. But this is, on the whole, unlikely. For quite a large part of the boom there will still be unemployment and thus money wages will tend to be rather insensitive to price rises. It is only in the later stages that money wages can be expected to rise at all rapidly. If a large rise occurs such that money wages rise by more than prices have risen over the earlier part of the boom, then from that stage onwards real wages may rise or at least will almost certainly fall by less than they would otherwise have done, for it may take time before prices rise in response to the rise in money wages. Recent experience however suggests that, taking account of the lengthy negotiation machinery for settling wage disputes, the price lag is likely to be much shorter than the wage lag. The most likely outcome therefore is that real wages will oscillate about a falling value, assuming that raw material prices are rising.

In the downswing raw material prices tend to fall relatively to money wages and that will tend to raise the real wage and share of labour and strengthen our conclusions of the previous section. But given that raw material prices are falling, any fall in money wages (downward shift in the supply schedule of labour) will have unfavourable effects on labour's share and real wage. This is especially true once cartelisation has increased and prices become more rigid.

We may sum up the conclusions of this section as follows.

1 Rising money wages in the boom and falling money wages in the slump will tend to counteract the factors operating on labour's real share and wages during these two phases of the cycle, which were discussed in the previous sections.

2 Since however raw material prices are rising faster than money wages in the boom and are falling more rapidly than the latter in the slump, the general direction of change in the share of labour and its real wage which we have come to expect is unlikely to be affected.

V

Throughout this chapter we have been discussing the share of wages defined in terms of labour's own product, and as a proportion of net output (total revenue). But for many purposes the share of wages in terms of wage goods is more important. Moreover, we must be careful when we attempt to fit our present micro-economic analysis into a macro-economic model.

If the structure of production and relative prices remained constant between boom and slump, there would be no problem, and we could proceed from micro- to macro- economic analysis without any difficulties. But the structure of production in a boom differs from that of the slump, for in the former the ratio of investment to output is high and in the latter it is low. It is therefore particularly dangerous to continue using aggregates to analyse this situation.

Unfortunately no more than classification is possible. If the marginal product of labour in the investment goods industries is higher than that in the consumption goods industries, then real wages in terms of consumption goods will tend to rise in the boom and fall in the depression. If the reverse is the case then real wages will tend to fall in the boom and rise in the depression. This is a question of fact and no *a priori* judgment is possible. It is however important to remember that this change in the structure of the economy may modify our arguments of the preceding sections. We shall return to this in the next chapter.

We must also now notice that the share of wages in income paid out will fluctuate far less over the course of the cycle than the share of wages in net income produced.[10] This is due to the fact that corporations seem to have a dividend policy such that the dividends fluctuate far less than do the total profits of the company. This factor also will be mentioned again in the next chapter.

Lastly we conclude this chapter by a brief survey of the facts as far as they are known. This will consist entirely in giving the findings of others, since no full scale statistical analysis can be attempted here. We wish however to stress that although the facts appear consistent with our theory they cannot 'prove' it. To do that we should have to have a full scale econometric model.

As far as the share of wages is concerned, there has always been some difficulty in separating salaries from wages. Both these however have tended to move in the same direction, so that the problem is not as great as might be feared.

Dunlop,[11] using a series of wages and salaries combined, has found that labour's share in both net and gross income has increased in every depression since 1919 and diminished in all booms since that date. The share of wages in income paid out, however, has remained approximately constant. Dunlop's chart is reproduced as Table 1, on the following page.

On the other hand, while Dunlop shows that 'the share (of labour) rose sharply in depressions' he adds the proviso that 'only major cyclical swings appear to influence substantially any share estimate'.[12] This is well in accordance with our own theory, for if fluctuations are small, changes in the slopes of the cost curves will be small and in any case stock decumulation may take the place of rising prices. Lastly, Dunlop found that 'those industries which lost weight most heavily in depressions showed the most marked increase in their rate of participation, (i.e. in the share of wages of those industries) in the same periods'.[13] This factor is clearly responsible for damping fluctuations in the share of wages.

When we come to real wages the best and most exhaustive analysis is that of Tsiang. He finds that

> 'In the United States as well as in Britain, product wage rates in the system as a whole (i.e. money wages deflated by a wholesale price index with trend removed), . . . appear to be on the whole positively correlated with the percentage of unemployment.'[14]

This however was not true for all industries taken separately, some of which, in the period 1919–38 and mainly manufacturing industries, appear to have had fairly constant product wages. But those are the industries which have a high rate of technological innovations and in which there are the largest number of new products. These findings therefore do not directly contradict those of our theory which was based on given production

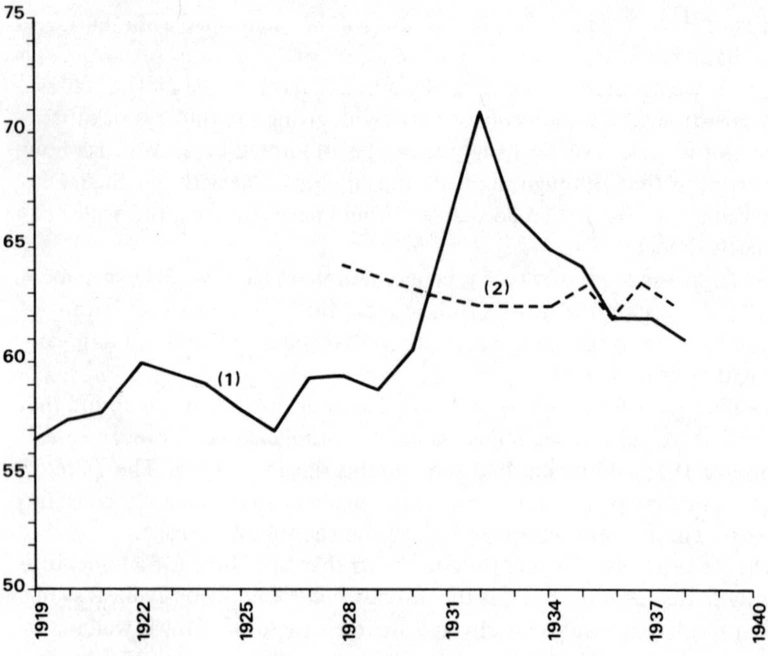

table 1. Labour's share in the national income and in income paid out (Dunlop, *Wage determination under Trade Unions,* page 157).

Denominator:

1 National Income with net savings adjusted. (Kuznets *National Income, and its Composition.* Table 22B, page 217).

2 Income paid out. (Department of Commerce).

Numerator:

Wages and Salaries.

functions. For the system as a whole however, as we have seen, our theory is consistent with the facts.

Tsiang also shows that there is a tendency for 'raw material prices to rise relatively to money wages when the level of employment and output rises and to fall when the level of output falls.'[15] As far as gross profit margins are concerned, no definite pattern seems apparent from the data. In the twenties gross profit margins were on the whole positively correlated with output, but after that the reverse was true for some industries. But the thirties were by all standards very exceptional even as compared with other slumps. It is significant that Tsiang finds that all those industries the gross profit margins of which rose in the depression had very rigid prices.[16] That is what we would expect from our theory.

The facts, scanty though they are, and briefly as we have listed them, at least do not contradict the general trend of the argument of this chapter. But it would be foolish to claim any great certainty for our conclusions. Any given movement in the share of wages depends on the exact magnitude of the changes in the parameters which determine it, and a theoretical analysis in the last resort can, in most cases, be no more than classificatory.

Chapter 9

The share of wages in the trade cycle: II

In the previous chapter we were mainly concerned with the effects of the trade cycle on the share of wages within an individual firm or industry. In this chapter an attempt is made to provide a macro-economic theory to complement the analysis up to this point. Two main problems will come up for consideration.

1 In what circumstances will producers be forced to produce on their short run marginal cost curves, a matter which we have up to now taken more or less for granted?

2 How does the ratio of consumption goods to output vary during the course of the cycle?

If we can answer 1) then we shall know in what circumstances to expect ϵ to exceed unity, and therefore, remembering what was said in the previous chapter, the share of wages to be below its long run equilibrium value (assuming constant returns to scale). If we can answer 2) then, remembering our discussion of the wage fund doctrines, we will have a rough general guide to the behaviour of the share of wages in terms of consumption goods during the cycle which will provide a check on the more detailed analysis based on the slopes of cost and revenue curves.

The most recent and, for our purposes, most useful analysis of the trade cycle is that of Hicks,[1] and although we shall not agree with all the propositions put forward by this author, our work is heavily indebted to his.

I

We shall first examine the rate of growth in the stock of capital during the upward phase of the cycle.

Hicks' theory of the upswing may be briefly given as follows. In the depression there is no induced but only autonomous investment, which is growing at a constant rate g. He designates this type of investment at any one moment of time by $H(1 + g)^t$. The income equation for the depression may now be written as

$$Y_t = cY_{t-1} + H(1+g)^t, \quad (9.1)$$

where cY_{t-1} is the output of consumption goods in period t and c is the propensity to consume. In depression equilibrium 9.1 may be written as

$$Y_t = L(1 + g)^t. \quad (9.2)$$

That is to say, incomes are growing at a constant rate, and the level of income is such that autonomous investment equals savings. Since according to 9.2 ($g > 0$) incomes are growing, the excess capacity left over from the previous boom gradually becomes smaller. When excess capacity has become zero, then induced investment will again appear. 9.1 now becomes

$$Y_t = cY_{t-1} + v(Y_{t-1} - Y_{t-2}) + H(1 + g)^t, \quad (9.3)$$

where v is the relation. 9.3 has the equilibrium solution

$$Y_t = E(1 + g)^t > L(1 + g)^t, \quad (9.4)$$

and incomes will rise. But Hicks assumes that 9.3 is explosive so that incomes will overshoot their equilibrium level $E(1 + g)^t$.

This is Hicks' theory of the upswing in brief. For the purpose of this section Hicks' theory of induced investment must be treated in a little more detail. Hicks maintains that

> 'induced investment in fixed capital can generally be thought of as depending upon changes in *actual* output; for the output which can be produced from a given equipment is capable of some variation within the Marshallian short period.'[2]

And again elsewhere he says explicitly that 'in the short period the enlarged output can be produced, but only by using the capital equipment at more than its optimum intensity'.[3] In addition Hicks assumes that the investment which takes place at period t will be such as will enable producers to produce the increase in output which took place between say period $t - 1$ and $t - 2$ at the optimum factor ratio, i.e. producers regard that increase in output (which was produced at a less than optimum capital intensity) as permanent. Expectations of future increases in output are thus wholly absent from Hicks' accelerator.

But Hicks is worried by the possibility that the increase in output made possible by larger capacity may be greater than the increase in output which induced the producer to enlarge his capacity.[4] He gets over this difficulty by pointing out that larger capacity does not necessarily mean producing up to full capacity. But this simply will not do. For if in period t investment is such as to produce an increase in output at optimum capital intensity greater than a past increase which induced the investment, then a subsequent increase in output (at less than the optimum factor ratio) will induce less investment than the previous increase, assuming both to be the same, for there is now some excess capacity. That is to say Hicks' explanation would lead him to a variable accelerator, while throughout his work it is assumed constant.[5]

We shall therefore assume first that the increase in output which can just be produced at the optimum factor ratio when induced investment has taken place is equal to the (past) increase in output which induced the investment. After all, we are assuming that the producer regards this increase in output as permanent. But we shall re-examine this assumption presently.

Writing ΔY_t^o as the increase in output at period t which can be produced in period t at the optimum factor ratio, and assuming that there is a one period lag between the time new investment goods are produced and the time they start contributing to output, and writing α for the marginal efficiency of investment, we have

$$\Delta Y_t^o = \alpha I_{t-1} = \Delta Y_{t-2}, \quad (9.5)$$

where I_{t-1} is the output of investment goods in period $t-1$ and ΔY_{t-2} is the increase in output produced in period $t-2$ at less than the optimum factor ratio. (The absence of a superscript "o" always denotes 'at less than the optimum factor ratio'.)

Dividing both sides of 9.5 by Y_t we have

$$\frac{\Delta Y_t^o}{\Delta Y_t} = \frac{\Delta Y_{t-2}}{\Delta Y_t}. \quad (9.6)$$

From 9.6 it follows immediately that if the rate of growth in output is constant ($\frac{\Delta Y_{t-2}}{\Delta Y_t}$ = constant) then the ratio of output at optimum factor ratio (optimum output) to actual output will also remain constant. But during the upturn the rate of growth of output is increasing ($\frac{\Delta Y_{t-2}}{\Delta Y_t}$ is diminishing) and hence the ratio of optimum to actual output is falling. This means that during the upswing (remembering that there is no excess capacity) producers will be forced to produce ever higher up on their short run cost curves. Remembering what was said in the previous chapter this will mean that the share of wages will fall below its equilibrium value[6] (given the elasticity of demand).

Given our assumption therefore which, Hicks' footnote notwithstanding, is also his (implied) assumption, we have shown that the share of wages will not only be less in the boom than in the slump, but will continue to decline during the upswing as long as the rate of growth in output is increasing.

But let us now drop the assumption of equation 9.5. If we assume that the short run cost curves are all approximately linear and that all demand curves are also linear, we can take account of the fact that the planned increase in output at optimum factor ratio may be greater than the actual (present) increase in output at less than the optimum factor ratio. In figure 8, LAC = LMC is the long run cost curve assuming constant returns

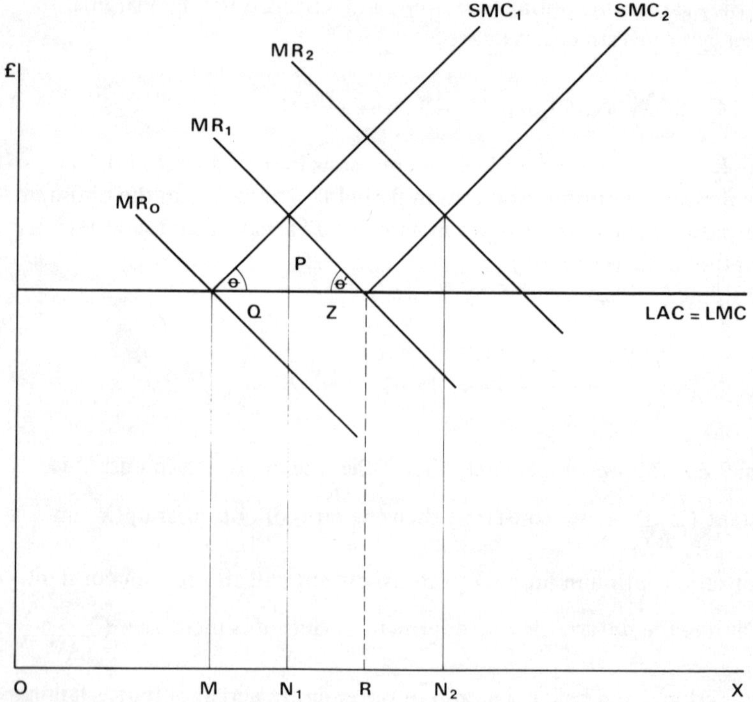

figure 8

to scale. SMC_1 and SMC_2 are a series of short run marginal cost curves. MR_o is the marginal revenue curve at the point when depression turns into boom. MR_1 and MR_2 are subsequent marginal revenue curves.

At the turning point output is equal to OM. In the next period there is an increase in demand which can only be met by employing more labour relatively to capital, i.e. by moving along SMC_1. Output will be increased by MN_1. But the optimum increase in output is given by MR. Producers will therefore invest sufficient to produce $OR > ON_1$ in the subsequent period. Now

$$Q \tan \theta = Z \tan \theta', \quad (9.7)$$

$$\frac{\tan \theta}{\tan \theta'} = \frac{Z}{Q}, \quad (9.8)$$

and it follows from 9.8 that the ratio of the additional increase in output forthcoming when investment has taken place to the increase in output when investment has not yet been undertaken remains constant as long as the slope of MSC_1 = the slope of MSC_2 and the slope of MR_1 = slope of MR_2 etc.

Making this assumption and assuming that this is true for all firms we can rewrite 9.5 as

$$\Delta Y^o_t = \beta \Delta Y_{t-2}, \quad (9.9)$$

where $\beta > 1$ and constant. As long as β remains constant (and as long as $Y^o_t < Y_t$) however, our previously reached conclusions remain intact, for once again the ratio of optimum to actual output will be diminishing as long as the rate of growth of actual output is increasing. Hence given increasing marginal short run costs and the elasticity of demand, the share of wages will be diminishing in the upswing, for given diminishing returns at full capacity, ϵ of the previous chapter will be increasing. That is to say the proportionate increase in labour needed to produce a proportionate increase in non-optimum (factor ratio) output is increasing.

The accelerator in the above case is such that producers invest in any one period an amount such that they are able in the subsequent period to produce an output greater than the current increase in output at the non-optimum factor ratio. Since however we assume that in the upswing demand is growing at an increasing rate or, more precisely, the demand schedule is shifting to the right by an increasing amount, they will find that in each period a certain part of output has to be produced at a non-optimum factor-ratio. They will therefore continuously invest, and provided the short run marginal cost curves and all the marginal revenue curves retain their old slopes and are linear and provided expectations remain the same the accelerator will remain the same.

But now two difficulties arise. 1) Hicks assumes all prices constant up to the ceiling (full employment) while we assume prices to rise and 2) will expectations remain the same? We shall deal with the second problem first.

It seems pretty clear that if the demand schedules are continuously shifting to the right, producers' expectations will become elastic, i.e. they will base their plans on the assumption that demand will be increasing in the future. This raises insurmountable difficulties as far as the formal mathematics of the analysis is concerned, for there is no general way known of dealing with difference equations with variable coefficients. But certain implications of elastic expectations can nevertheless be examined in a more or less intuitive fashion.

The essential point is that producers had not been anticipating increases in demand in the early stages of the boom. Hence when expectations become more elastic, induced investment demand will increase. This will mean an increase in aggregate demand by more than it would otherwise have increased. Hence if producers have been extrapolating past rates of increases in demand into the future (which they might) they will again find that they have underestimated the increase in demand. It is therefore quite possible that in spite of anticipatory investment they will continuously find themselves forced to produce on their short run marginal cost curves. I think it is fairly certain that anticipatory investment *need not* imply that producers are always producing at their optimum factor ratio.

We now come to the second stage of our argument. We have seen in chapter 6 that if producers are always producing at the optimum factor ratio, certain equilibrium conditions must hold. But we have already assumed the expansion equation to be explosive such that incomes will overshoot their equilibrium level. We have thus two alternatives: either we assume that because of changes in expectations we eventually reach that constellation of coefficients (propensities and marginal efficiencies) for which incomes are 1) at their equilibrium level and 2) expanding at their equilibrium rate, or we do not reach this particular constellation. In the latter case either incomes continue to overshoot the equilibrium level, or the boom comes to an end.

I have found it impossible to provide a rigorous analysis of the likelihood of any of the above-mentioned eventualities occurring. But on *a priori* grounds the equilibrium result seems the least likely. For that would imply that the boom from then onwards is purely maintained by elastic expectations, i.e. even though producers have all the capital they require to produce current output they nevertheless continue to invest in anticipation of further increases. I do not think that many major booms were of this type.

The possibility of elastic expectations leading to a slump appears to me also not very great, although overinvestment may of course occur. Much here depends on the production and construction lags. In any case this eventuality is not very troublesome for our analysis since, until the slump is reached, incomes will be expanding at a rate greater than the equilibrium rate.

If incomes continue to expand at a faster rate than the equilibrium rate as defined in chapter 6, then by definition producers will continue on their short run cost curves. But we cannot now say whether the ratio of optimum to actual output will be increasing, constant or diminishing.

The introduction of expectations as an explicit variable into the analysis, it is seen, makes it difficult to reach any very precise conclusions. On the whole however our main proposition that producers will be producing on their short run cost curves through at least the greater part of the boom seems to hold. It must moreover be remembered that expectations are only likely to have significant effects when the boom has lasted for some time, so that for a considerable part of the boom the assumption of constant expectations will probably do little violence to the facts.

We may sum up our conclusions to this stage.

1 Provided prices are not rigid and producers equate short run marginal cost to marginal revenue, and provided expectations are not elastic, the ratio of output which can be produced at the optimum factor ratio to the output actually produced will diminish as long as the rate of growth in output is increasing.

2 Given that there is no excess capacity as normally defined, 1) implies diminishing returns to labour and therefore increasing output elasticity of demand for labour ϵ, during that part of the boom for which the assumptions under 1) hold true.

3 Therefore if the elasticity of demand is constant, the share of wages in the boom will not only be less than in the slump, but will be diminishing throughout the boom for which our assumptions hold.[7]

4 This result is subject to all the qualifications discussed in the previous chapter under the heading of rising money wages and raw material prices.

5 When expectations become elastic it is just possible that an equilibrium in the sense of chapter 6 may be established. Our results would then only hold as long as such an equilibrium had not been reached.
6 If elastic expectations do not lead to 5), we may still expect the share of wages to be lower than in the slump, but we cannot be sure that they will continue to diminish.

We now turn to the second problem raised above, namely that of prices.

II

If elastic expectations are troublesome to formal analysis, changing prices are even more so. But I cannot share the implication in some writers' work that such price changes should therefore be neglected. Whatever may be said for this attitude when analysing changes in aggregate income, it is useless for an analysis of distribution. I cannot therefore understand Hicks (who assumes constant prices over the major part of the cycle) when he says 'most of the distribution changes between large classes which take place during the cycle, are in my view themselves a part of the "lag" process and have therefore been implicitly taken into account'.[8] Since not only all prices but all coefficients are assumed constant I have been unable to find the distribution changes 'implied' by Hicks' analysis.

Moreover, I find the assumption of constant prices difficult to digest. Let us look at Hicks' theory in greater detail for guidance on this point.

Hicks assumes the following adjustment process. In period t there is an increase in demand. Being unexpected it leads to a decumulation of stocks equal to that increase. Output therefore remains constant. In the subsequent period t + 1, output increases by the amount of the increase in demand in period t. But since demand is continuously increasing stocks will be continuously decumulating.[9] We can easily find a stock equation from Hicks' assumptions.

Using the notation of previous chapters we write

$$C_t^d = cY_{t-1}^s, \quad (9.10)$$

implying that the consumption demand in period t is a function of yesterday's output. That is to say the revenue from decumulated stocks is not treated as disposable income.

Next we have

$$I_t^d = v(Y_{t-2}^d - Y_{t-3}^d), \quad (9.11)$$

assuming that there is a two period reaction lag so that investment demand today is proportional to the day before yesterday's increase in demand. We therefore have the demand equation

$$Y_t^d = cY_{t-1}^s + v(Y_{t-2}^d - Y_{t-3}^d). \quad (9.12)$$

Now Hicks' assumptions imply that

$$Y_t^s = Y_{t-1}^d. \quad (9.13)$$

We therefore rewrite 9.12 as

$$Y_t^d = cY_{t-1}^s + v(Y_{t-1}^s - Y_{t-2}^s), \quad (9.14)$$

and our supply equation, remembering 9.13, therefore becomes

$$Y_t^s = cY_{t-2}^s + v(Y_{t-2}^s - Y_{t-3}^s). \quad (9.15)$$

This is the Hicksian output equation, with autonomous investment neglected (since it does not affect the argument). Subtracting 9.15 from 9.14 and putting $Y_t^d - Y_t^s = \Delta_t$ and again remembering 9.13 so that we can always substitute an appropriate Y^d for any Y^s we have

$$Y_t^d - Y_t^s = \Delta_t = c\Delta_{t-2} + v(\Delta_{t-2} - \Delta_{t-3}). \quad (9.16)$$

9.16 is our 'decumulation of stocks' equation. It is seen that it is in all respects similar to 9.15 the output equation, so that if 9.15 is explosive 9.16 is explosive. That being the case I cannot believe that producers are willing to have ever-increasing stock deficits, quite apart from the probability that they will soon have no stocks to decumulate.

The likelihood that prices will in fact rise, making Hicks' assumptions, seems very great indeed. It is true that we cannot be certain that they will rise to a level at which marginal short run cost is equal to marginal revenue. It is true that rising prices may themselves affect our equations which are couched in real terms.[10] But I think it would be a mistake to attempt to be too precise. What we have shown is that prices almost certainly will rise, so that at least the direction of change in the share of wages indicated in the previous section, subject to the qualifications we made there, will be correct.

III

There is yet an alternative approach to the problem we have set ourselves, which we have outlined in chapter 7, and which will also clear up some of the formal difficulties involved in price changes.

In the depression the ratio of consumption goods to total output may be written as

$$\left(\frac{C}{Y}\right) = \frac{cL(1+g)^{t-1}}{L(1+g)^{t}} = \frac{c}{1+g} \quad . \qquad (9.17)$$

But in the depression the only investment is autonomous investment. Once the upturn has commenced there will also be induced investment, but as long as the rate of growth of autonomous investment remains the same, the ratio of consumption goods to total output in boom equilibrium will be the same as in depression equilibrium.[11] We have however assumed that when the boom gets under way incomes will overshoot their equilibrium level. Hence during the boom g', the actual rate of growth at any one moment of time, will exceed the equilibrium rate of growth. This will mean that the ratio of consumption goods to total output will be below its equilibrium level during the upswing.

Let us examine this proposition in greater detail. Using the notation of chapter 7 we have

$$c_t^s = c_{t-1}^d \cdot \frac{Y_{t-1}^s}{Y_t^s} \quad , \qquad (9.18)$$

which gives us the ratio of consumption goods supplied to total output at any one moment of time. If c^d can be assumed constant, we know already that during the upswing $\frac{Y_{t-1}}{Y_t} < \left(\frac{Y_{t-1}}{Y_t}\,_e\right)$ (where the subscript e refers to the equilibrium ratio) since $g' > g$ at any one moment of time so that $c_t^s < (c_t^s)_e$ at any one moment of time. But can we assume c^d constant? We have argued elsewhere in this book that if the (marginal) propensity to consume of wage-earners is unity, and non wage-earners don't consume anything, the share of wages[12] in the national income will diminish, provided prices are flexible, when c^s diminishes. This will also be true when wage-earners' (marginal) propensity to consume is less than unity, but greater than the positive (marginal) propensity to consume of non wage-earners, provided these propensities remain the same. But if a lower c^s implies a lower $\frac{W}{Y}$, then clearly c^d will not remain constant.

How will this affect our argument? Whenever prices are flexible and money wages are not, or lag behind prices, then price increases during the upswing will tend to have a damping effect on the rate of growth in output, for the fall in the share of wages will lead to a reduction in the propensity to consume (c^d). Hence at the same time as c diminishes, $\frac{Y^s_{t-1}}{Y^s_t}$ will tend to increase. We cannot therefore be certain that c^s will continue to diminish during the upswing. But we can be certain that c^s will be below its equilibrium value. This can be seen as follows.

Given constant (marginal) propensities to consume of wage-earners and non wage-earners, there will correspond one (constant) propensity to consume for the community as a whole to each distribution of income, such that the lower the share of wages, the lower also the community's propensity to consume. From this it follows that if prices are flexible and $c^s_t = c^s_e$ (the proportion of income supplied in consumption goods in depression equilibrium), $\left(\frac{W}{Y}\right)_t = \left(\frac{W}{Y}\right)_e$. But that must mean that $c^d_t = c^d_e$ (the depression equilibrium propensity to consume). Hence we have in period t + 1

$$c^s_{t+1} = c^d_e \cdot \frac{Y^s_t}{Y^s_{t+1}}, \quad (9.19)$$

from which it follows that if $c^s_{t+1} = c^s_t = c^s_e$, $\frac{Y^s_t}{Y^s_{t+1}} = \left(\frac{Y^s_t}{Y^s_{t+1}}\right)_e$; that is to say the rate of growth in income will have to be the same as the depression rate of growth of income. But we already know that if $c^d = c^d_e$ the rate of growth in income in the upswing will be greater than that in the depression and we therefore conclude that $c^s_{t+1} \neq c^s_e$. Moreover $c^s_{t+1} \not> c^s_e$, for this would imply that the rate of growth in income is less than in the depression, i.e. that the downswing had started, while we are concerned with the share of wages in the upswing. We therefore conclude that $c^s_{t+1} < c^s_e$ so that $\left(\frac{W}{Y}\right)_{t+1} < \left(\frac{W}{Y}\right)_e$. Hence if rising prices, by damping the rate of growth in income, lead to a constant rate of growth, it will be at a lower share of wages than that appropriate to depression equilibrium.

But there are several qualifications to this conclusion.

1 If as has recently been suggested the propensity to consume is not only a function of current income but also of the previous highest income, then the proportion of income demanded in consumption goods will decline, so that c^s may fall without causing a rise in prices and thus a fall in $\frac{W}{Y}$.

2 In so far as entrepreneurs anticipate increases in demand, prices will rise by less than they would otherwise have done, and may conceivably not rise at all, although that is unlikely.

Subject to these qualifications we may say the following.

1 The share of wages in the upswing will be less than its equilibrium value, because the ratio of consumption goods to output is below its equilibrium value.

2 There will be one stage in the upswing when the rate of growth in output is increasing in spite of rising prices, and for that stage the share of wages will continuously fall below its equilibrium value. Later rising prices will tend to reduce the rate of growth in income, and the share of wages will rise again, but as long as the upswing continues the share of wages will remain below its equilibrium value.

In the downswing the share of wages will tend to increase for the following reason: g, the rate of growth in output, is negative. Hence $\frac{Y^s_{t-1}}{Y^s_t} > 1$ while during the upswing the reverse was the case. But during the upswing we have seen that, under certain assumptions, $\frac{W}{Y}$ will be below its equilibrium value, and in equilibrium $\frac{Y^s_{t-1}}{Y^s_t} < 1$. Therefore, making the same assumptions and remembering equation 9.18, c^s_t will be above its equilibrium value and so therefore will the share of wages.

IV

We are now ready to sum up our conclusions concerning the share of wages in the trade cycle. Given that there are no innovations and that production functions are linear and homogeneous, there will in general be one value of $\frac{W}{Y}$ which is compatible with equilibrium in a progressing economy. This was examined in chapter 6. In the upswing of the trade cycle the following factors will tend to lower $\frac{W}{Y}$ below its equilibrium value.

1 Because of the time it takes to increase production, when demand increases, and because there will be little or no excess capacity during the upswing, producers will find themselves forced to produce on their (rising) marginal short run cost curves. This means that the output elasticity of demand for labour will be above its equilibrium value and therefore by equation 8.5 the share of wages will be below its equilibrium value.
2 During that part of the upswing for which the rate of growth in output is rising it can be shown that the ratio of 'optimum' (minimum long run cost) output to actual output will diminish, and hence given diminishing returns, the share of wages will continue to decline below its equilibrium value as ϵ rises above its equilibrium value.
3 Since the rate of growth in output in the upswing exceeds its equilibrium value, the ratio of consumption goods to total output will fall below its equilibrium value. Given the assumptions made throughout this book, the share of wages in terms of consumption goods must fall below its equilibrium value.
4 During that part of the upswing for which the rate of growth of output is increasing, the ratio of consumption goods to total output will be diminishing and therefore the share of wages will continue to decline below its equilibrium value.
5 In the boom the marginal disutility of production is equated to marginal net profit and in the slump to marginal gross profit. Hence it is likely that the net profit margin in the boom will exceed that in the slump, provided the elasticity of demand remains constant.
6 Rising raw material prices.
7 A possible fall in the elasticity of demand.

The following factors will tend to counteract the tendency for $\frac{W}{Y}$ to fall below its equilibrium value during the upswing:

1 Rising money wages.
2 A possible increase in the elasticity of demand.
3 Elastic expectations, although these will only tend to limit the extent to which $\frac{W}{Y}$ falls below its equilibrium value, but are unlikely to prevent such a fall altogether.
4 A sharp fall in the marginal disutility of production due to increased optimism.
5 Rigid prices, so that all or part of excess demand is met out of stocks

throughout. Again, while prices are not as flexible as we have assumed, they are unlikely to be completely rigid. Thus this factor will damp the fall in $\frac{W}{Y}$ without altogether preventing it.

The following factors will tend to raise $\frac{W}{Y}$ above its equilibrium value in the downswing.

1 The fact that the marginal cost of using capital is now zero or nearly so will mean the labour intensity of production will be below its equilibrium level. Given constant returns to scale, the depression prime cost curve will lie below the long run cost curve and the share of wages will be equal to $1 - \frac{1}{e}$. But in long run equilibrium (when constant long run marginal cost equals marginal revenue) the share of wages and capital together is equal to $1 - \frac{1}{e}$. Hence if e is constant, the share of wages in the depression must be above its equilibrium value.

2 Since the rate of growth is negative, while in equilibrium it is positive, the ratio of consumption goods to output will be above its equilibrium value.

3 Falling raw material prices.

4 A possible increase in the elasticity of demand.

5 The fact that marginal disutility of production is now equated to marginal gross and not to marginal net profits, i.e. a likely fall in the 'exploitation coefficient'.

Factors tending to counteract the rise in $\frac{W}{Y}$ above its equilibrium value.

1 Price rigidities. These are unlikely to be such as to prevent the rise in $\frac{W}{Y}$ altogether.

2 A large increase in the marginal disutility of production. This is unlikely because of the increased need for liquidity.

Looking through this summary it is seen that while it is impossible to be completely certain that $\frac{W}{Y}$ will be above its equilibrium value in the slump and below it in the boom, the reasons for expecting this to be the case[13] are very strong.

But we have left one important factor out of account altogether – the impact of innovations. It is to this that we must now turn our attention.

Chapter 10

Innovations and the share of wages (historical)

Many economists have in the past devoted their attention to the problem of innovations. It is therefore proper that before we attempt an analysis of our own some of the main theories on this topic should be examined. This chapter is accordingly devoted to a survey of these theories. This survey is not intended to be exhaustive. We shall only examine some of the more important of the theories that have been advanced in the past.

This chapter is a digression in more ways than one. For most attention in the past has been concentrated on the effects of innovations on employment and less attention devoted to their effects on the distribution of income. A survey of most of the theories put forward must therefore necessarily devote its main attention to the 'employment effect'. But as we shall see, once we know what was said about the employment effect of innovations we shall by implication also know what was thought about their effect on the distribution of income.

The authors considered in this chapter are: Ricardo, Wicksell, Alvin Hansen, N. Kaldor, J.R. Hicks, and Robinson. These writers' theories on the whole represent pretty accurately the main trend of thought on this subject over the last hundred years or so.

I

Ricardo's opinion of the effect of inventions is presented in his celebrated chapter 'On Machinery'.[1] Ricardo starts the discussion by renouncing the opinion which he says he had previously held that

> 'an application of machinery to any branch of production as should have the effect of saving labour, was a general good, accompanied only with that portion of inconvenience which in most cases attends the removal of capital and labour from one employment to another'.[2]

He declares that he is now 'convinced that the substitution of machinery for human labour is often very injurious to the interests of the class of labour', although he still believes it (the invention) to be advantageous to 'the landlord and the capitalist'. What has brought about Ricardo's conversion?

Prior to his conversion Ricardo believed that both money profits and money rents would remain constant, after the invention had been adopted, so that a fall in price brought about by a superior method of production would clearly increase the real income of both landlord and the capitalist. (The constancy of money profits is assumed by competition, but no reason is given for assuming money rents constant.) Further, nothing has happened to change the quantity of 'circulating capital' so that even though money wages remain constant the capitalists' 'power of demanding and employing the same quantity of labour is as great as before'. Now the elasticity of demand for the particular commodity in the production of which the improvement has taken place, may not be great enough to assure the continued employment of all workers concerned in its production. But the general elasticity of demand for all sorts of consumption goods is high, for, says Ricardo, he (Ricardo) has ever been impressed by the fact that

> 'the desire for food is limited in every man by the narrow capacity of the human stomach, but the desire of the conveniences and ornaments of building, dress, equipage, and household furniture, seems to have no limit or certain boundary'.[3]

That being so, the displaced workers will easily find employment elsewhere. Money wages and employment thus remaining constant, and prices falling, it is clear that the real total share of wages will have increased.

The flaw which Ricardo detects in this earlier reasoning of his is primarily the assumption that the quantity of circulating capital and thus the power to demand labour remains constant. This, he says, is a special assumption which will only be fulfilled if productivity is raised to such an extent as 'to afford in the shape of net produce as great a quantity of food and necessaries as existed before in the form of gross produce'. If this assumption is not fulfilled some labour will definitely be made redundant. This conclusion is reached as follows: by the doctrine of the wage fund, the capital of the community is at any one moment divided between fixed and circulating capital, the latter being available for support of labour during the period of production. Let C_1 and C_2 represent fixed and circulating capital respectively and let $C_1 + C_2 = K$ equal to the total quantity of capital in existence at any one moment of time. An invention will increase C_1 and given K, must of necessity diminish C_2. Therefore unless, as a result of the increased productivity, K subsequently increases by at least the same amount by which C_2 has diminished, the fund available for the employment of labour will have diminished, and some labour will therefore become redundant.

Now G (gross produce) = C_2 + NP (net produce, i.e. output added). If therefore C_2 diminishes without a corresponding increase in NP, gross product will diminish as a result of the increased use of machinery. Thus

> 'an increase in the Net Produce of a country is compatible with a diminution of the gross produce and . . . the motives for employing machinery are always sufficient to ensure its employment if it will increase the net produce, although it may and frequently must, diminish both the quantity of the gross produce and its value.'[4]

Ricardo's theory of the effect of invention on employment is illustrated in the diagram (figure 9), on the following page. On the horizontal axis of the right hand part we measure employment, on the upper vertical axis C_2 (circulating capital), on the left hand horizontal axis C_1 (fixed capital) and on the remaining axis NP (Net Produce). Since by the doctrine of the wage fund the level of employment is given by $\frac{C_2}{W}$ where W equals wages, the relationship, given the level of wages, between C_2 and W is linear, and is represented by the curve OW. The line K_1K_1, shows the possible combinations of C_2 and C_1 with a given amount of capital K_1. II is a constant product curve. The combination of C_2 and C_1 will be such as to yield a maximum product, i.e. where K_1K_1 is tangential to II, that is at Q_1.[5] We shall assume that the production functions are linear and homogeneous throughout. Hence once the optimum combination of C_2 and C_1 has been reached, this ratio, in the absence of inventions, will remain constant. We can then use C_1 as an index of K_1. The curve OS_1 shows how the supply of C_1 varies with NP, where C_1 is regarded as an index of K. The shape of this curve and its position are thus determined by two factors: a) the propensity to save on the part of capitalists and b) the given ratio of C_1 to C_2.

Let us now suppose that before the invention, the level of employment was given by ON_1, the amount of C_2 and C_1 by OM and OT respectively and the amount of net produce by OP_1. Let there now be an invention which increases the use of C_1 of a given capital K_1. This is represented by a change in the constant product curve to PP with a new optimum combination of C_2 and C_1 as shown at Q_2. If nothing further happened the level of employment would fall to ON_2. But there has been an increase in net product. Let the new value of the latter be given by OP_2. Since the ratio of C_1 to C_2 has increased we must shift the OS curve downward. (Perhaps this needs further elaboration: suppose the ratio of C_1 to C_2 was

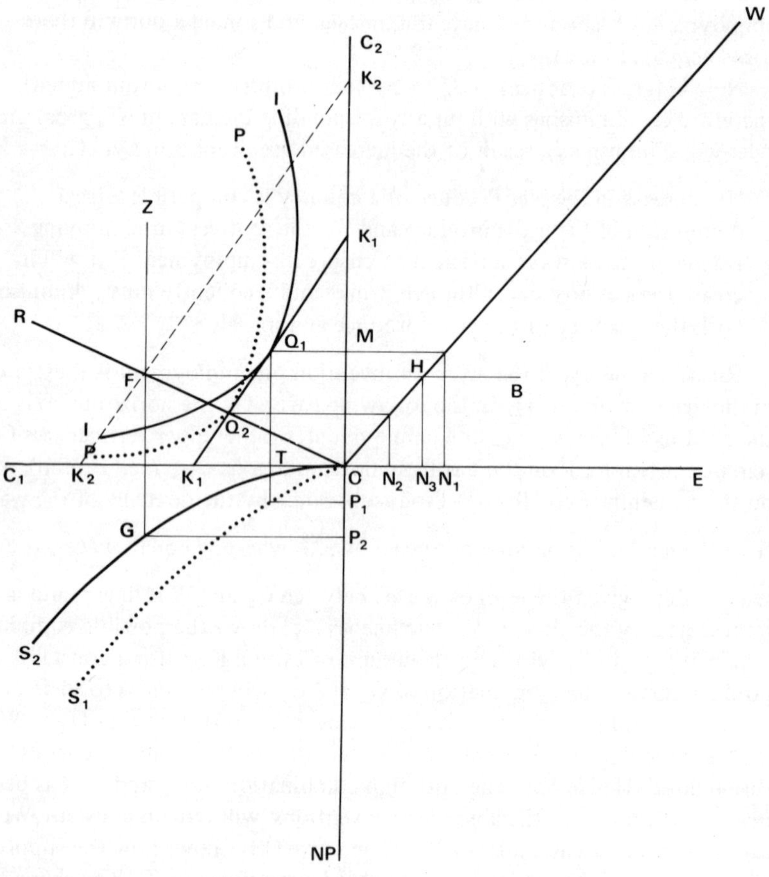

figure 9

1 : 3 before the invention, then to denote an increase of 4 units in K, we would have to increase C_1 by one unit. If the ratio after the invention has changed to 2 : 3, then to denote an increase in K by 4 units we would have to increase C_1 by approximately 3·05 units, i.e. we must lower the OS curve.)

The new position of the OS curve is given by OS_2. Draw P_2G parallel to the x axis, and draw GZ vertically to the x axis to intersect OR at F. The slope of OR measures the new ratio of C_1 to C_2. We now draw K_2K_2

through F to denote the increase in K. By drawing FB parallel to the x axis to intersect OW at H we can find the final level of employment ON_3. This is less than the level of employment before the invention.

The effect of the invention on the level of employment thus depends primarily on two factors: 1) the increase in net produce and 2) the capitalists' propensity to save. We have left out of account the capitalists' propensity to spend on 'menial services' part of their increased net produce and thus to raise employment. The higher this propensity the better are the prospects from the point of view of labour. It will be noted that the invention Ricardo considers is always of a 'labour saving' type.

But in spite of the danger that unemployment may follow an invention, Ricardo is careful to add that we should not infer from what he has said that he believes 'that machinery should not be encouraged'. This, because his analysis started from a position of stationary equilibrium which was suddenly disturbed by the invention. In fact, however, in a progressing economy, the accumulation of capital is continually proceeding, so that inventions determine how the newly saved resources should be employed, rather than changing the use of already 'saved up' resources. Moreover, 'machinery and labour are in constant competition' and the former will frequently not be employed until the rise in population and capital and thus the rise in the cost of subsistence and hence wages has made that profitable. Lastly even though the increase in NP and the new saving therefore are initially insufficient to re-employ all the labour dismissed, these savings are performed periodically (with every income period, Ricardo says annually) so that sooner or later a fund of sufficient magnitude to re-employ all the labour must be accumulated.

In the next chapter we shall again have cause to mention Ricardo's theory. But it should be noted that as it stands, even though its terminology could not be accepted today and its mode of analysis is based on the doctrine of a 'wage fund', it nevertheless reaches conclusions well in accordance with modern theory. If out of any given output producers decide to invest more without consuming less, prices will rise and, given the money wage, real wages will fall. Once the investment has been completed prices will fall again, but the marginal productivity of capital is now either higher than that of labour, or it has remained the same, but more capital per unit of output is employed. Hence capitalists' share in income has increased and the effect of this on employment will depend on what capitalists do with this higher share. Since, in Ricardo, savings were equivalent to investing funds, it follows that the greater proportion of their income capitalists invest, the further to the left will K_1K_1 be pushed (see figure 9) and the higher will the level of employment be.

This of course is a pretty free translation of Ricardo's theory, but his remark that since savings continue to accumulate employment will increase again seems to imply this interpretation. But we must be careful to remember that investing in this context means investing not only in capital goods – but also in circulating capital – i.e. investing funds in general. Therefore as long as the innovation by raising the rate of profit (net product) increases the rate of investment (in the above sense) above what it would otherwise have been, employment may be maintained or may increase.

II

Ricardo's theory was vigorously attacked by Wicksell,[6] who maintained that a possibility of a reduction in the gross produce due to technical improvement envisaged by Ricardo was 'theoretically untenable' under the assumption of free competition. Wicksell's argument rested on two important assumptions: 1) that under free competition the total physical product (assuming a single good) will always be maximised and 2) that money wages will always fall to such a level as will ensure the employment of all available labour.

Given these assumptions it easily follows that a technical improvement (labour saving) will always increase the gross total product. For the technical improvement in any industry A must necessarily lower costs there (otherwise it would not be employed), and thus raise profits. This will attract new entrants from other industries until prices in A have fallen to the extent necessary to ensure tangency between the cost curve and the (horizontal) demand curve in each unit of production there. Since at that point average costs are at a minimum it follows that physical product in the original industry is at a maximum.

At the same time (unless the elasticity of demand for the products of A was very high) some labour will be displaced from there (A). This will lower wages and thus increase the attractiveness of more labour – intensive industries which will expand (because of higher profits) and re-employ the surplus labour. At the end of the processes (which occur simultaneously) the physical product in each industry must be a maximum. But by definition the maximum physical product after the invention must exceed the maximum before it. Therefore gross product has increased and 'Ricardo has failed to draw the final conclusion from his own assumption'.[7]

Wicksell's argument may be shown diagrammatically as follows. In the diagram (figure 10) the horizontal distance O_1O_2 measures the total amount of labour available. The left hand vertical axis measures wages, equal to the marginal product of labour in industry B, while the vertical axis on the right hand side measures the marginal product of labour in A (which also measures the wage and is equal to it). The curves DD and dd are the demand curves of industry A and B for labour respectively. The line $W_1 W_1$ measures the level of wages and may be regarded as the supply curve of labour. Under the assumption that all available labour is employed and that free competition prevails, $O_2 M$ labour will be employed by A and $O_1 M$ by B. Let there now be an invention in A such that any given output can be produced with less labour. Unless the demand for the final product is of an extremely high elasticity (in which case there is no problem) the curve DD will fall to $D_1 D_1$. Wages remaining constant $O_2 L$ will be employed by A and $O_1 M$ by B leaving LM workers unemployed. This will lower the wage and continue to do so until a wage OW_2 is reached such that $W_2 W_2$ passes through the point of intersection of $D_1 D_1$ and dd at Q. At this lower wage $O_2 N$ ($< O_2 M$) will be employed by A and $O_1 N$ by B

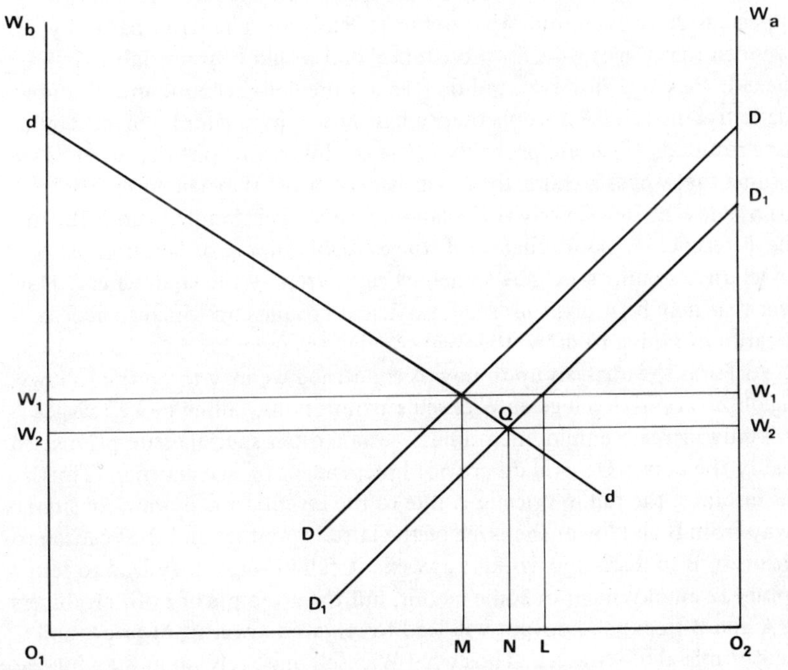

figure 10.

and all labour will once again be absorbed.

That the total output will have increased after the reabsorption of LM needs no proof, it being assumed by the adoption of the invention. It will be noticed that at the end of the process envisaged by Wicksell the wage-earners are relatively worse off for 1) the total income has increased without an increase in employment and this will tend to reduce the share going to wages and 2) while the money incomes of capitalists and landlords has remained constant in spite of falling prices, the money income of wage-earners has diminished. Thus it is no wonder that Wicksell is forced to confess that

> 'this maximisation [of product] may well be associated with and even conditioned upon a reduction in the distributive share of one of the factors of production, in this case labour'.

He also points out 'that this shows a serious error of those who see in free competition a sufficient means for the satisfaction of the needs or desire of all members of society'.[8]

Independently of the merits of Wicksell's analysis up to this stage, he appears to have been somewhat unfair to Ricardo. The latter naturally assumed that wages were at 'subsistence' and would thus not fall any further. If they did, however, fall then as our previous account and diagrammatic treatment of Ricardo's theory has shown, no unemployment would have resulted. Wicksell, probably aware of this, points out that even 'if we assume that wages are already at subsistence level' they can in reality 'remain below it, indefinitely if the labourers and their families can make up the difference by poor relief' or if 'the available supply of labour must, under any circumstances, be somehow supported by the landowners'. However that may be it does not seem sufficient grounds on which to accuse Ricardo of failing to draw 'the final conclusions from his own assumptions'.

As far as the analysis up to now is concerned we may make the following observation. Even given Wicksell's assumptions, falling money wages will only increase employment under certain other special assumptions. In reality the curves DD and dd are not independent of one another. Thus, for instance, the fall in price in A due to the invention will draw consumers away from B and lower the price of the latter's product and thus cause producers in B to discharge workers as well. A fall in wages may lead to temporary re-employment of some labour, but the attempts of both producers in A and B to expand output will lead to renewed lowering of prices and thus dismissal of workers. Thus what Wicksell must rely upon is an increase in the aggregate demand, due to a fall in the general level of prices. For this to occur certain special assumptions concerning the quantity of nominal money, expectations etc. are necessary which are not specified by him (see post). These objections, however, do not apply if A and B are only a very small part of the total demand for labour. But then it is difficult to interpret what is meant by 'the quantity of labour available' and Wicksell's equations 2) and 3) have no meaning. Lastly it may be noted that by using these two equations, i.e. by assuming full employment before and after the invention, Wicksell has assumed away much of the problem.

We may conclude this examination of Wicksell's analysis by briefly surveying the alternative route by which he attacks the problem of invention, especially the effect on the share of wages in the national product.[9] This alternative route is closely connected with Wicksell's theory of capital. Wicksell as an exponent and refiner of Böhm-Bawerk's theory of capital believed in the doctrine of the wage fund. Whereas, however, the classicals had regarded wages as determined by simply dividing the wage fund K which was regarded as given, by the available supply of labour A, Wicksell allowed for a period of investment and wrote $W = \frac{2K}{tA}$; i.e., the wage fund was, under continuous input-output relation, only required to support labour during half the period of investment (production). Under perfect competition the rate of wages, the rate of interest and the period of investment were determined simultaneously by the condition that wages and interest are maximised.

Now given K and A, anything which increases t (the period of investment) will *ceteris paribus* reduce wages as is shown by our equation above. Thus any invention which increases the attractiveness of long term investment will increase the vertical time dimension of any given quantity of capital, and thus bring about a reduction in the 'quantities of accumulated labour and land employed each year (period)'. At the same time 'there will also be a reduction in that part of current land and labour which must be saved and capitalised each year to renew that which is consumed'. The quantity of current labour will, other things being equal, increase and thus the marginal product (wage) of current labour may well be reduced. An increase in savings (capital) on the other hand will reduce the current labour available and thus tend to increase its marginal productivity and hence the famous conclusion that 'the capitalist saver is . . . fundamentally the friend of labour, though the technical innovator is not infrequently its enemy'.[10]

It is seen that Wicksell comes to the same conclusion by both methods of analysis. It should, however, be noticed that in that part of his analysis which we have just examined he has failed to state rigorously the conditions which must be fulfilled in order that the share of wages in the national income be diminished. He was content to say that

> 'this [the increase in current labour] need not necessarily cause their [labour] marginal product and share in the product to be reduced, since the total product has simultaneously been increased by the technical discovery, yet a reduction may clearly result'.

We may sum up Wicksell's analysis in the following way. A labour-saving innovation raises the marginal productivity of funds invested with a low rate of turnover relatively to the marginal productivity of funds with a rapid turnover. This means that labour's wage will have to be reduced (since wages have a rapid rate of turnover) if unemployment is not to arise. Once again the assumption is made that a fall in wages will automatically increase employment. It is then possible, as we shall see later in this chapter, that the share of wages may increase. But it is difficult to see how this is possible if the amount of labour employed before and after the innovation is the same (as assumed by Wicksell). For unless the ratio of capital to labour is actually diminished, a rise in the share of wages would imply a fall in the marginal product of capital relatively to that of labour, and that Wicksell does not assume to happen.

Wicksell's celebrated conclusion that the capitalist saver is frequently the friend of labour simply means that if capitalists invest more, the demand for labour will increase. Here his conclusions are essentially similar to those of Ricardo.

III

Let us now turn to more recent analysis of the effect of inventions on employment. The contention that in a competitive system inventions could not lead to permanent unemployment was attacked by Alvin Hansen.[11] Unfortunately Hansen's analysis was ambiguous and could be answered relatively easily by the defenders of the Say-Wicksell school of thought. Nevertheless it contained much which since its publication has been made familiar by Keynes. It is therefore worthwhile to examine Hansen's article in some detail.

Hansen assumes conditions of absolutely inelastic demand. The introduction of labour-saving machinery will a) lower costs and prices and b) displace some labour. The consumers gain in purchasing power, but the quantity sold is not increased because the consumers' gain *'is offset by the loss in purchasing power suffered by the displaced workers'.*[12] There is thus no 'net gain in purchasing power'. Thus, while 'the purchasing power is sufficient to maintain the former demand for goods despite the reduced purchasing power of the displaced wage-earners', it is not sufficient to maintain the former demand for labour. Hansen thus maintained that the fall in the share of wages, by reducing consumption demand, would keep aggregate demand constant, whereas the increased output made possible by the invention required an increase in aggregate demand if employment was to remain constant. But to reach this conclusion he assumed money wages to remain constant throughout (which may be a reasonable assumption) and confessed that if this assumption were not fulfilled, the surplus labour would be reabsorbed.

But under Hansen's assumption, as Kaldor points out,[13] 'the existence of "permanent" employment will depend upon the assumption of rigidity of money wages and not on the nature of the invention'. Hansen's case is therefore by so much weakened since the school of thought which he attacks never maintained that there would be no permanent unemployment following an invention if money wages remained constant. As we have already seen both Ricardo's and Wicksell's analysis would show permanent unemployment in this case. In fact, however, as we shall show presently, the fall in money wages need not be sufficient to ensure the re-employment of the displaced labour.

To return to Hansen's analysis. The fall in prices due to the fall in cost will clearly increase the real quantity of money $\frac{M}{P}$ (where M = the quantity of cash and P = index of prices). Given the real demand for cash balances, an increase in $\frac{M}{P}$ will cause people to transfer some of their idle into active balances, i.e. they are likely to buy securities. This will lower the rate of interest and will increase the supply of bank credit and the entrepreneur's demand for it, since it enables him 'to put the productive forces in motion in anticipation of the sale of the product out of which the factors of production would eventually have to be paid'. This may be put in more recent terminology as, the increased quantity of real money will, given the community's liquidity preference, reduce the rate of interest and the amount of (nominal) money (M) held. The latter will be made available for credit expansion.

'Thus at the same time that the labour saving improvements displace labour, the accompanying reductions in prices displace credit. The

> released credit leaves a means by which the displaced labour can be re-absorbed'.[14]

Hansen therefore acknowledges that falling interest rates may do the work normally attributed to falling money wage rates in re-employing labour.[15]

He further shows that the rate of interest may fall even if there is no fall in prices due to the reduction in costs. This because the increased profits then earned will lead to an increase in 'investment in the general capital market'. Thus there are two forces at work, on the one hand the reduced share of wage earners will lead to a fall in consumption demand, while on the other hand, the increased share of profits will lead to an increase in savings (supply of credit) which will reduce the rate of interest. If the falling rate of interest makes new investment profitable, output will expand and labour will be re-employed.

Hansen's analysis may be illustrated diagrammatically as follows. In figure 11 the horizontal axis of quadrant A measures the output of consumption goods (C) and the vertical axis the output of investment goods (I). T_0T_0 and T_1T_1 are two transformation curves drawn on the assumption of the full employment of labour, before and after the invention respectively. The horizontal axis of quadrant B measures the rate of interest (r) and the curve II relates the demand for investment to the rate of interest. The vertical axis of quadrant C measures price (P), and the curve RP shows the relationship between the rate of interest and the level of prices, assuming M, the nominal quantity of money, to be given. The curves W_0W_0 and W_1W_1 in quadrant D show how the demand for consumption goods varies for different levels of prices, given the total money wage bills W_0 and W_1 before and after the invention respectively.

Let us suppose that before the invention the level of prices was equal to OP_0, the wage bill equal to W_0, the rate of interest equal to OR_0, the level of investment OI_0 and the output of consumption goods OC_0. After the invention T_0T_0 shifts to T_1T_1, and total money wages fall to W_1. Now if the reduction in aggregate demand due to the fall in W is to be exactly counterbalanced by the increased demand due to a fall in price (the rate of interest and investment remaining constant) prices must fall to OP_1 in order that consumption demand remains at OC_0. This, however, must mean unemployment, since OC_0 and OI_0 lie on T_0T_0 which now represents a less than full employment level of output.

But the lower prices will cause interest rates to fall to OR_1 and this will increase investment demand and thus employment. Money wages remaining constant W_1W_1 will now shift back to W_0W_0 since the total money wage

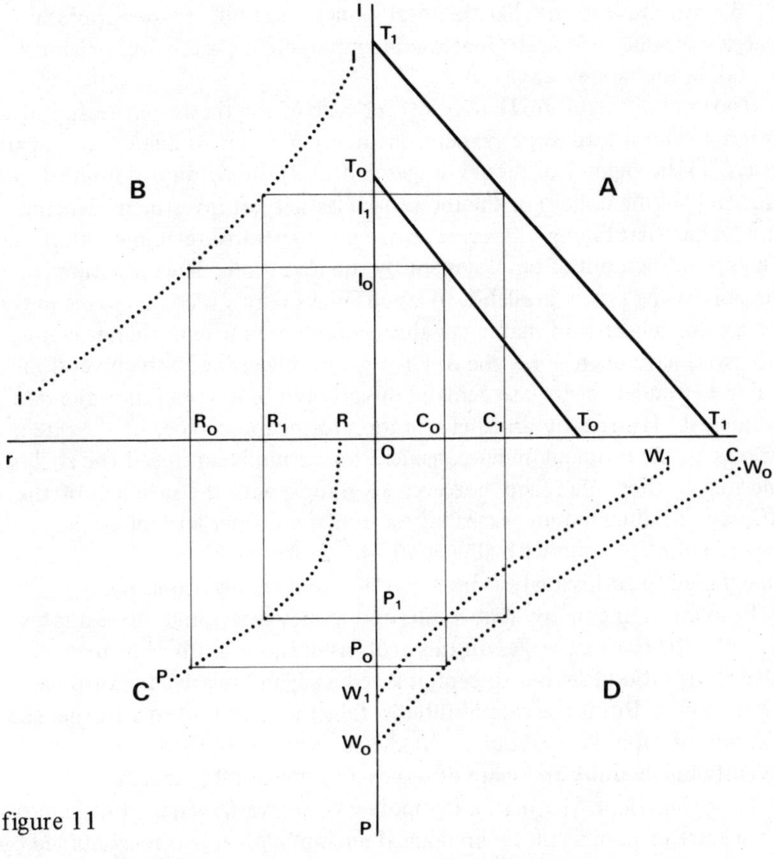

figure 11

bill will once again increase. If all labour is re-employed, the level of investment will be given by OI_1 and the output of consumption goods by OC_1. It is seen from the diagram that OI_1 and OC_1 lie on $T_1 T_1$, the transformation curve appropriate to full employment output after the invention. It is further clear from the diagram that if the rate of interest were price-inelastic (i.e. if M varies), or the demand for investment interest-inelastic, that re-employment of labour could only take place if wages fell. For if wages fall, prices will fall and that will, given the elasticity of the curve $W_1 W_1$, increase the demand for consumption goods. It is true that if money wages fall, the total wage bill will also diminish and thus shift W W to the left. But Hansen clearly assumes that a fall in wages will increase demand by more (by decreasing prices) than it will diminish it by decreasing

W. We can thus assume that the total money wage bill remains approximately constant at W_0, the increase in employment exactly outweighing the fall in the money wage.

To sum up, therefore, Hansen's scepticism of the thesis that technical progress cannot lead to permanent unemployment seems due to two separate issues: 1) the rigidity of money wages and/or 2) the rigidity of interest rates (due to banking policy) or the interest-inelasticity of investment demand, or a feeling that falling interest rates are insufficient to re-employ all those who are thrown out of employment by the invention. The reduction in the purchasing power available to labour plays only a secondary role in his theory, namely that of making re-absorption more difficult than it would otherwise have been – i.e. the original fall in prices due to the invention will not stimulate aggregate demand directly but only via a fall in the rate of interest. Hansen, by drawing attention to the importance of the rate of interest to the problem under consideration certainly advanced the analysis one step further. He failed, however, to grapple with the problem of the efficacy of falling money wages in restoring the former level of employment, and in common with almost all who wrote on this subject at that time, failed to fit his analysis into that of a progressing economy.

In so far as unemployment results and money wages and interest rates are rigid, the share of wages on this analysis must diminish. For to each output the ratio of labour to capital is reduced, and relative factor prices are the same. But if the rate of interest falls this may lead to a further substitution of capital for labour and if the elasticity of substitution is sufficiently below unity the share of wages may conceivably increase.

The problem of whether falling money wages were sufficient to banish the spectre of permanent technological unemployment was re-examined by Kaldor, writing about the same time as Hansen.[16] The long run elasticity of demand for labour can only be zero, writes Kaldor, if

> '1) the technical coefficients be fixed and either 2) the proportions of capital and labour are the same in all industries or 3) the elasticity of demand for the products of all industries which employ relatively more labour should be less than 1)'.

If these conditions are not fulfilled (and they are not likely to be) falling money wages must increase the profitability of labour – using as opposed to labour – saving processes, and some of the labour which had been thrown out of work by the invention will be re-employed.

This, however, seems far too simple a view of the problem. In the event of variable coefficients a fall in the general level of money wages will tend to lead to a substitution of labour for capital everywhere. If prices are flexible, then the steep fall in the demand for investment goods will lower their price and put a stop to the substitution. Thus, unless the price of capital goods is not flexible, we cannot rely on 'the substitution effect' for our re-employment of labour. If the coefficients are fixed in the various industries and reliance must therefore be placed on a movement of firms from capital intensive to labour intensive industries, then to the objection just mentioned must be added the undoubted fact that the period in which a 'reshuffling' is accomplished is likely to be fairly long. Therefore numerous variables such as changes in the quantity of money, new inventions etc. which could otherwise be regarded as constant, must now be taken into account.[17, 18]

But if little reliance can be placed on the substitution effect even less can be placed on the expansion of output due to the falling costs as a result of the invention. Kaldor maintains that we can only assume a technical invention to have no effect on output if we assumed that 1) it is known to one firm only, 2) that this firm had a complete monopoly, and 3) that marginal cost (i.e. the slope of the total cost curve) remains constant. These assumptions are unlikely to be fulfilled and therefore, concludes Kaldor, the fall in cost must necessarily lead to an increase in output. This, however, is erroneous. Unless the part of the economy affected by the invention is very small, the demand curve is not fixed and given. Falling prices due to the expansion of the industry affected by the invention will lead to a substitution of that industry's output for the output of other industries, and unless their prices are rigid, lower their price, and thus shift the demand curve of the first industry to the left. Thus, even though marginal cost is reduced, marginal revenue may be reduced in the same proportion (unless other causes operate). Moreover, falling costs need by no means lead to an attempt to increase output if entrepreneurs are aware of the interdependence of their prices with those of others.

Thus falling costs due to the invention or to a reduction in money wages need not lead directly to an increase in output unless the lowering in the general level of prices leads to either 1) reduced interest rates and increased investments and/or 2) increased demand for consumption goods. Falling money wages need not lead to much substitution of labour for capital even if Kaldor's conditions for 'non-substitution' are not fulfilled. The attempt to solve the problem by a partial analysis only is doomed to failure, unless the part of the economic system affected be very small. Kaldor makes no such provision. But if the part of the economy is very small, unless there is no loss of employment in that part, and then there is no problem, money wages must fall and under the implicit assumption of the homogeneity of labour, the whole system will be affected.

Chapter 11

The effects of innovations on the share of wages: further analysis

In the foregoing chapter we were mainly concerned with a historical review of the various theories that have been employed in the past to analyse the effect of inventions on the level of employment and the share of wages. It will have been noticed that all the economists with the exception of Hansen, who maintained that labour-saving inventions would not lead to a fall in employment, postulated a fall in real wages. By Wicksell this assumption is made explicitly, by Ricardo implicitly and Kaldor again makes it explicit. Since then an invention will by definition increase the productivity of the community's resources and since employment does not fall, the total national income will be increased at the same time as real wages fall. It is clear therefore that the share of wages will also diminish.

This analysis however, as we have seen, leads us into difficulties. For one thing it assumes that real wages will always fall to that level at which full employment is established. This assumption has become increasingly untenable, for as was shown by Keynes it involves the further assumption that labour can control its own real wage and this is not correct without further assumptions. On the whole it seems to be agreed among modern economists that, for instance, falling money wages will in a closed economy, and given the interest-elasticity of investment demand, affect real wages only to the extent to which they tend to lower the rate of interest.

But an even greater drawback of most of the theories discussed in the previous chapter is that they are wholly couched in terms of comparative statics. But innovations or technical progress surely belong to the field of economic dynamics *par excellence.*[1] The use of comparative statics seriously obscures the path of adjustment, it takes little account of the impact of obsolescence, and it always assumes that some "long run" equilibrium will be established – which need not be the case. But all these raise important problems and any theory which ignores them can only deal with a very limited aspect of what is involved.

Our efforts in this chapter will accordingly be devoted to discussing some of these problems which have hitherto been ignored. We shall proceed in three main stages. First we shall assume that the rate of growth of output is constant and given, and examine the impact of innovations in that situation on the share of wages. We will then examine the effect of innovations on the share of wages over the trade cycle. Lastly we shall briefly discuss the effect of differing rates of innovations (and thus rates of growth in output) on the secular movements of the share of wages.

I

Let us suppose that incomes are growing at a constant (geometric) rate. Let us also assume that the working population is constant and given. Then in the absence of innovations, full employment must be reached sooner or later.[2] Once that is the case, the ratio of capital to labour (or what Marx calls the organic composition of capital) will grow. Owing to the workings of diminishing returns this will mean that before long the share of wages will change. It will also mean that the ratio of investment in any given increase in output will grow. Both these then are incompatible with continued equilibrium.

If the share of wages is to remain constant while the rate of growth in output also remains constant, 1) the rate of growth in capital (K) must equal the rate of growth in income and 2) the proportionate increase in capital in each period must equal the proportionate fall in the ratio (R) of the marginal product of capital to the marginal product of labour in each period. We can therefore define an equilibrium 'type' and rate of innovation.

Since in the absence of innovations R would probably be diminishing faster than K is increasing (owing to a diminishing elasticity of substitution) the innovation will probably have to be labour-saving in Hicks' sense. Conditions 1) and 2) state the rate of innovation must be such that a) the elasticity of substitution is kept equal to unity through time and b) the rate of growth in capital is kept constant. These conditions are of course no more than we would expect.

But let us now suppose that the rate of innovation is below the equilibrium rate. That will mean that the rate of growth of capital will exceed the rate of growth of income and that the rate of growth in R will (probably) exceed the rate of growth in K.[3] The latter would lead us to expect the share of wages to rise.[4] But since the rate of growth in capital now exceeds the rate of growth in income, the proportion of income invested in each period is increasing. Hence if the constant rate of growth in output is to be maintained with a rate of innovations below the equilibrium innovation rate, the share of wages must *fall* and *not* rise as we would have been led to expect from a consideration of the production function alone. For at the old share of wages demand will exceed supply in each period and prices will therefore rise, and if the constant rate of growth in output is to be maintained prices must rise relatively to wages.

Similarly if the rate of innovation is above the equilibrium rate, R will tend to increase by less than K, and K will grow at a slower rate than income. The first consideration would lead us to expect a fall in the share of wages. But the ratio of investment to output is falling through time. Hence if the constant rate of growth is to be maintained the share of wages must increase. This will come about by an excess of supply over demand in each period and the consequent fall in prices. If the constant rate of growth is to be maintained prices must fall relatively to money wages.

But all our conclusions refer to a situation in which the rate of growth in output remains constant. But unless the rate of innovation is the equilibrium rate, the rate of growth in output is unlikely to remain constant. In particular, rising and falling profit margins will influence the willingness to invest and supply output and thus the rate of growth of output will be altered. Moreover many innovations are made not when there is full employment but, on the contrary, in the slump. Clearly the effect of innovations will not be the same if we do not assume the rate of growth in output constant.

II

If we were only interested in comparing two dynamic equilibrium positions, the analysis of Hicks and Robinson would be most useful. For in dynamic equilibrium as we have defined it in this book producers are on their long run cost curves and *ex ante* demand is always equal to *ex ante* supply. Hence the effect of an innovation on the distribution of income, given 'the degree of monopoly', will depend only on the relative prices of the factors and on the form of the new production function. In this case whenever the distribution of income changes we must assume the rate of growth of income to have adjusted itself to the new distribution, such that the ratio of consumption goods to output is equal to the new (*ex ante*) propensity to consume.

But it is difficult to believe that this sort of 'comparative dynamics' is at all useful or realistic – in fact if anything it is even further removed from reality than an analysis based on stationary states. This section is therefore devoted to an analysis of the effects of innovation on distribution when dynamic equilibrium is not assumed.

Once the assumption of equilibrium is dropped, and a macro-economic analysis attempted, it will be found that the ratio of investment to income will give us the best guide in examining the effect of innovations on the distribution of income. For given the consumption functions of individuals and groups and assuming, as we have done throughout this book, that a lower (marginal and average) propensity to consume for the community as a whole implies a lower share of wages and *vice versa* for a rise in this propensity, the changes in the investment ratio will give us an indication of changes in the distribution of income in terms of consumption goods.

Moreover, since the absence of dynamic equilibrium implies the trade cycle, we must examine the effects of innovations on the investment ratio in the framework of the cycle.

Now in a depression, the only investment is autonomous. This type of investment need not be dependent on innovations. If it is not dependent on innovations,[5] then the occurrence of the latter need have no effect on either the ratio of investment to output or on the rate of growth of output in the depression. For it is conceivable that producers are continuously replacing old with more efficient capital so that net investment other than autonomous investment remains at zero. This however is very unlikely.

In general, I think it more realistic to assume that the making of innovations coincides with the end of the depression. For 1) producers will not innovate if there is large excess capacity, 2) producers will not innovate if uncertainty is high and thus innovations will tend to coincide with an improvement in producers' expectations, 3) innovations have 'complementarity' effects by a) making other innovations profitable and b) by forcing other producers to innovate as well. Because of these reasons we shall henceforth assume that innovations made in the depression will mark the end of the latter and the beginning of the upturn.

We have already seen that innovations made in full employment equilibrium, if they are equilibrium innovations, will be such as to keep the ratio of investment to output constant. We now generalise this concept to define a neutral type and rate of innovations as that type and rate of innovations which will leave the ratio of investment to output $\left(\frac{I}{Y} = i\right)$ at every moment of time, the same as it would have been in the absence of innovations.[6] Our full employment equilibrium innovation is then a special case of a neutral innovation.

We now assume, for the reasons given above, that innovations occur in a depression only when all excess capacity has been exhausted. Hence if we use Hicks' theory of the upturn,[7] the latter occurs at the same time if innovations take place or not. Now, in the absence of innovations, and using Hicks' assumptions, there will be a definite time path in the ratio i which corresponds roughly with that of incomes. In depression equilibrium the ratio is constant. During the upturn i will be increasing as long as the rate of growth in output is increasing. In general i will start to decline again before the downturn, owing to a slowing down of the rate of growth in output. During the downswing i will continue to decline until it is once again stabilised in depression equilibrium. A neutral innovation will be one which leaves this time path of i unaffected.

Now it is easily seen that a neutral innovation as defined, must leave the share of wages at the same value at any one moment of time as it would have been in the absence of innovations. For, given that there are no changes in the consumption function of individuals, if the ratio of investment to income is the same as it would have been in the absence of innovations, then the ratio of consumption goods to income will be the same as it would have been without innovations, and continuing to assume flexible prices that will mean that the course of the share of wages over the trade cycle will be unaffected by the innovation.

This must be true whatever the effect of the innovation on the marginal productivity of labour and capital. Consider for instance the case where the innovation is capital saving (raises the marginal product of capital relatively to that of labour) and where in consequence the ratio of total wages to total payments made to capital increases. We have seen that some theorists regard this as sufficient indication that the share of wages will rise. But if the innovation is neutral in our sense, then the share of wages in terms of consumption goods *cannot* rise above what it would otherwise have been. This simply means that the prices of consumption goods will rise, and profit margins increase, until the share of wages is at the value it would otherwise have had.

But in what circumstances will an innovation be neutral in our sense? Let us first examine the upswing.

In the upswing an innovation can only be neutral in our sense if 1) it leaves the capital intensity of production unchanged or 2) if the increase in investment demand due to obsolescence offsets the fall (if any) in investment demand due to a lower optimum capital intensity of production or 3) if the rate of growth of output increases whenever the optimum capital intensity of production diminishes.

1 Given the prices of the factors of production the optimum capital

intensity of production can only remain unchanged by the innovation if the latter is labour-saving in Hicks' sense and is such that the new constant product curves are parallel to the old constant product curves along lines drawn vertically to the capital axis. If that is the case then our innovation will be neutral during the upswing, provided the rate of growth of output is not affected by the innovation. If the rate of growth in output is higher than it would have been in the absence of innovations then i will be higher than it would otherwise have been and *vice versa* if the rate of growth in output diminishes.[8]

2 If an innovation is such that the new total cost of production is less than total prime cost then it will pay producers to scrap their old equipment. But not all innovations need be of this sort. It is for instance perfectly feasible that every time a producer wishes to make an *addition* to his equipment, i.e. invest, he will purchase a type superior to his present machines without scrapping the latter. This will always be possible as long as it is feasible to produce with a plant consisting of different types of machines performing the same service. In that case the obsolescence demand may well be zero, and old machines will simply be replaced by superior ones, when the former have worn out or are fully or at least partially amortised.

There is thus no simple way in which to estimate the obsolescence demand caused by any particular innovation. If this demand is zero and 1) does not hold, then we can say straight away that the innovation cannot be neutral in our sense. The upswing will be less steep and the ratio of consumption goods to output greater than it would otherwise have been. For an innovation to be neutral it must therefore be of a type such that it pays producers to replace at least part of their old equipment by new before the former is due for replacement anyway.

But it may now be asked, will not an innovation of that type lead to a sudden jump in investment demand (due to obsolescence) in one period and then fall off again? I think not. For an innovation made in some firms will cause others to innovate as well. If we conceive the innovation to be spreading gradually from firm to firm as other producers become aware of it and realise its advantages, obsolescence demand may be increasing from period to period. Thus it is conceivable that obsolescence demand may just offset the fall in investment (due to higher productivity) which would otherwise occur in each period. But clearly this would be in the nature of a fluke. It is thus possible that an innovation may be neutral for part of the upswing but not over the whole of the latter.

3 If the rate of growth in output increases when the optimum capital

intensity of production diminishes then the ratio of investment to output may remain constant even if obsolescence demand is zero. This follows immediately if we remember that investment in any period t which is neither autonomous nor obsolescence investment is proportional to the rate of growth in output. If then an innovation for instance makes for more elastic expectations, or induces some producers to invest who would not otherwise have invested, the rate of growth in output may increase so that even though the optimum capital intensity of production has diminished the ratio of investment to output remains the same as it would have been in the absence of innovations.[9]

Whenever 1), 2) or 3) or some combination of these factors is present, the innovation will leave the share of wages during the upswing at the same value it would otherwise have had.

Let us now examine the depression. We know that in depression equilibrium, when *ex ante* supply is equal to *ex ante* demand, producers will be equating marginal prime costs to marginal revenue, since there is excess capacity. If the 'degree of monopoly' associated with depressions is unaffected by the innovation, the share of wages will be the same as it would have been in the absence of the innovation if the ratio of raw material costs to wage costs in the depression is unaffected by the innovation. Hence our innovation will be neutral with respect to depression equilibrium if these two conditions are fulfilled: 1) the depression equilibrium degree of monopoly remains constant and 2) the depression equilibrium ratio of raw material to wage costs remains constant.

If our innovation is also to be neutral with respect to the downswing, i.e. before the new depression equilibrium has been reached, then this requires that the ratio of autonomous investment (the only investment assumed to take place in the downward phase and depression) to income is unaffected by the innovation.

If then an innovation made at the lower turning point is neutral with respect to one complete cycle, the share of wages during the course of the latter will be the same as it would have been in the absence of the innovation. But this does not mean that the innovation will be neutral over all subsequent cycles.

At the lower turning point after the one at which the innovation was made producers will, as already stated, be in momentary long run equilibrium as normally defined. In that position the share of wages will be determined by the orthodox factors of marginal productivity and profit margins. Let us call the lower turning point at which the innovation was made A and the lower turning point after that B. We can then make the following classification assuming no further innovations to take place.

1 If at B the share of wages $\left(\frac{W}{Y}\right)_B$ at which producers are in long run equilibrium is less than $\left(\frac{W}{Y}\right)_A$ the share of wages at which producers were in long run equilibrium in A before the innovation, then the average value of $\frac{W}{Y}$ over the cycle will now tend to be less than it would otherwise have been if

a) the optimum capital intensity of production is now higher and the average rate of growth of output the same or greater than in the previous cycle, or

b) the optimum capital intensity is the same but the average rate of growth in output is higher in A than in the previous cycle.

If a) or b) is not fulfilled then even though the equilibrium share of wages has been reduced by the innovation, the actual share of wages over the cycle may be higher than it would have been in the absence of the innovation, or it may remain constant.[10]

2 If $\left(\frac{W}{Y}\right)_B > \left(\frac{W}{Y}\right)_A$, then the average value of $\frac{W}{Y}$ over the cycle will be greater than it would otherwise have been if

a) the optimum capital intensity of production is now less and the average rate of growth of output is the same or smaller than in the previous cycle, or

b) the optimum capital intensity is the same, but the average rate of growth is smaller than in the previous cycle.

Unless either a) or b) is fulfilled then even though the equilibrium share of wages has increased, the actual share of wages over the cycle may be less than it would otherwise have been.

3 Where $\left(\frac{W}{Y}\right)_B = \left(\frac{W}{Y}\right)_A$, i.e. where the equilibrium share of wages has remained the same, the actual share of wages over the cycle will only remain the same if the average rate of growth of output is such that i is the same for cycles with and without the innovation. That is to say the innovation must not only be neutral over the cycle in which it is made but over all subsequent cycles.

Lastly if the innovation is not neutral with respect to the cycle in which it is made then the share of wages over that cycle, which we might conveniently call the 'adjustment cycle' will tend to be different from the share of wages in subsequent cycles, if no further innovations are made. There are thus two stages in the effects of innovations on the share of wages. First there will be the adjustment effect which will coincide with one complete cycle and which will largely depend on the effect of the innovation on the investment ratio i. Obsolescence demand is likely to be of major importance here. Secondly the innovation is likely to affect the course of all subsequent cycles and the equilibrium distribution of income. Here again the investment ratio will be of major importance. But so of course will be the equilibrium distribution of income.

The equilibrium distribution of income will determine producers' actions when out of equilibrium. Thus for instance the greater the divergence of the actual share of wages from its equilibrium share, the more abnormal will profits be and thus the greater the inducement to expand or contract incomes as the case may be. Unfortunately as in so much of our work, since variable coefficients are involved it has been found impossible to give a rigorous statement of our theory.

But I think it will be clear that the equilibrium theories of the effects of innovations on the distribution of income are inadequate, not only because they assume equilibrium when this need never be achieved, but also because they use a partial analysis of the firm to derive propositions which are to apply to the whole economy. If an innovation implies that on the average the proportion of income invested is higher than it would otherwise have been, then unless the consumption functions of individuals and groups of society change, so that for the same distribution of income the propensity to consume for the community is reduced, the distribution of income in terms of consumption goods must alter.

To most of us of the younger generation of economists brought up on Keynes' *General Theory* this proposition will appear strange at first sight. We have all come to believe that the burden of any adjustment will normally fall on the level of income and not on prices or the distribution of income. But when the static Keynesian theory is dynamised it becomes apparent that the level of income at which with a constant (marginal) propensity to consume, *ex ante* savings are equal to *ex ante* investment may never be reached, or if reached will only be maintained for a short time. Until such a stage is reached a higher proportion of income invested must necessarily mean, because of lags in production etc., a lower proportion of income consumed. Our assumption of flexible prices then ensures a change in the distribution of income in terms of these consumption goods. This assumption is the same as that made by Keynes who always assumed producers to be maximising their profit at every moment of time.

If the above analysis is correct then we are nearer to Ricardo than to such modern economists as Robinson. For as we have seen Ricardo paid great attention to the effect of the innovation on the ratio of circulating to fixed capital, i.e. the ratio of consumption to capital goods in the modern sense. Of course we do not wish to take over Ricardo's theory of employment nor his assumption that saving is equivalent to investing. What we do wish to take over, however, is the importance Ricardo ascribed to the ratio of consumption to investment goods. Any innovation has two effects: 1) it will affect the equilibrium ratio of the marginal products of factors to the ratio in which they are combined in production and 2) it will affect what we might loosely call the propensity to invest and therefore the share of wages when the system is not in long run equilibrium.

Modern economists seem to have been preoccupied with 1). This as we have seen is only admissable when comparing two systems which are both in dynamic equilibrium. Since however the same economists seem to believe that the typical capitalist economy is continuously subject to trade cycles, the assumption of continuous equilibrium does not seem very helpful. Once the assumption is not made 2) must be taken into account.

III

Up to now we have been concerned with the effect of a single group of innovations made at a particular moment of time. But in the real world it appears that certain long periods are marked with a stream of innovations, occurring at either regular or irregular intervals. Since long periods are involved, and since all sorts of innovations are made, it is impossible to give any precise analysis of the effect of such a stream of innovations on distribution. But the analysis of the previous section enables us to lay down the following general principles:

If the working population is given and constant then, 1) if the stream of innovations is such as to reduce the average investment ratio, the share of wages will tend to be greater than it would have been in the absence of innovations, and 2) if the innovation stream raises the average investment ratio, then the share of wages will tend to be less than it would have been in the absence of innovations.

This latter case is, I think, of special importance. Periods of intense innovation will tend to be accompanied by a high rate of obsolescence and, on the average, a greater investment demand than would otherwise have been the case. During most of the last century when there was a very considerable stream of innovations, thrift was considered a great virtue since the number of investment outlets was large. There can probably be little doubt that much of the classical theory of the wage fund was appropriate to this situation. For there was a continuous tendency for the investment ratio to rise and (since population was also increasing) for the real wage of labour to remain low. In retrospect of course we find that real wages as well as incomes rose considerably during that period, but so did the stock of capital. But whatever the effects of the innovations of that period on the relative marginal productivities of labour and capital, the average ratio of investment to income does certainly not appear to have declined and probably increased. Unless the capitalists' propensity to save increased this does imply that the share of wages could not have risen, and probably declined.

In a rapidly expanding capitalist economy, as Marx I think rightly conceived, the share of wages is kept low because of the high proportion of income which, on the average, is invested. It matters little in this connection that Marx, in common with other classical economists, held a fallacious theory of value. What is important is the simple fact that in any one period a community cannot at the same time invest and consume more. If innovations are such that the proportion of any income devoted to investment on the average is increasing, then the proportion of income devoted to consumption will be diminishing and this, in practice, will imply a fall in the share of wages.

We conclude therefore that modern theory no doubt has a superior *equilibrium* analysis of distribution. As far, however, as problems of economic development are concerned, the odds are greatly in favour of the classical theory.

IV

We may sum up our conclusions as follows.

1 In comparing two positions of dynamic equilibrium, before and after the innovation, the modern analysis in terms of the production functions, as outlined at the end of the previous chapter, is most appropriate.

2 Comparing dynamic or stationary equilibria does not seem very helpful.

3 If such comparisons are not made, and a macro-economic theory attempted, the effect of the innovation on the investment ratio, i, will be the most important as far as the distribution of income is concerned.

4 Innovations are intimately linked with the trade cycle and must be

analysed in the framework of the latter.

5 The effect of a particular innovation can be analysed in two stages: a) the 'adjustment effect' which will be spread over one complete cycle and b) the final effect.

6 Only neutral innovations, i.e. those which keep i constant, will leave the share of wages at the value it would have had without the innovation during the adjustment phase.

7 The final effect of the innovation will depend on a) the new equilibrium share of wages, b) the new equilibrium capital intensity of production, and c) the new average rate of growth of income over the cycle. It is perfectly possible for the equilibrium share of wages to increase while the actual share of wages diminishes.

8 A long period of more or less continuous innovations, if it is accompanied by a rise in the average investment ratio, will tend to reduce the share of wages even though the equilibrium share may be rising. Obsolescence demand is likely to be of special importance during such a period.

This concludes our analysis of innovations. There remain certain problems connected with the very long or secular period to which we now turn.

Chapter 12
Some further long run problems

Our discussion of the effects of innovations on the share of wages has led us from relatively 'short run' problems to a discussion of secular or long run influences on the distribution of income. Unfortunately however modern theory, with a few notable exceptions, has paid relatively little attention to these wider issues and at the time of writing there is no agreed body of general doctrine on this topic.[1]

This comparative lack of interest in the problems of economic development is probably due to the increasing specialisation of economists and their preoccupation with purely 'economic' matters and hence a reluctance on their part to explore fields which are frequently in the no-man's-land which constitutes the frontiers of the social sciences. Quite apart from this, there is the widespread feeling, at least on the part of non-Marxist economists, that our historical development is not purely mechanically determined, so that the search for 'laws of development' is bound to lead to failure.

Even if we were able (which we are not) to construct some sort of theory of economic development, this clearly is not the place to attempt it, and since no ready-made theory is available, we shall have to content ourselves in this chapter with a discussion of some very general principles in so far as they affect the distribution of income in the long run.

I

If there were no innovations and no population growth then before long the secular rate of growth of income would tend to zero. This however does not mean necessarily that we shall reach the classical stationary state with zero net investment and saving, for there may still be a trade cycle.[2] But the average stock of capital, level of employment and income will all be constant. In such a situation there are also no secular variations in the share of wages although the latter may of course still vary over the trade cycle.

Secular changes in the share of wages will therefore be mainly due to innovations[3] and population growth. Some writers when discussing such changes have concentrated their attention on what happens to the share of wages in an individual firm or industry when innovations take place or changes occur in the supply of labour, and then have applied their 'partial' theory to the whole economy without further ado. This as we have already had many occasions to note is illegitimate not only because of the purely technical problem of aggregation involved, but also because a macro-economic analysis brings out certain influences on the share of wages which are altogether ignored in the micro-economic analysis.

As long as we stick to the two special cases of economic development, the stationary state or the regular progressing economy, these difficulties do not arise. Both these special cases have this in common: the share of wages ruling in any one period will also be the share at which producers have maximised their utility (profits). Expectations are always fulfilled and the *ex ante* and *ex post* share of wages are equal. Once these two special cases are abandoned however this is no longer the case. In particular, the actual share of wages at any one moment of time may then move in the opposite direction to the share of wages which would rule in complete equilibrium.

The actual share of wages at any one moment of time is the outcome of a large number of complex and inter-related decisions taken at some previous moment of time. On the basis of the profitability of innovations, past unforeseen changes in demand, expectations, factor prices etc., certain individuals will demand a certain quantity of investment goods. On the basis of similar factors and past decisions, the consumption and investment goods industries will produce a certain output in a given period. Given flexible prices, there will be an *ex post* propensity to consume which is equal to the actual ratio of consumption goods to total output produced. The share of wages in terms of consumption goods in the given period will then be such as to bring about this *ex post* propensity to consume. Unless all expectations are fulfilled the *ex ante* propensity to consume will not equal the *ex post* propensity and the *ex ante* and *ex post* share of wages will also differ. In the light of the experiences of producers during the period certain new decisions will be taken and the process will continue. In a world of lagged reactions, and of discrete construction periods, there is no reason why this process should end in equilibrium when *ex ante* and *ex post* values are equal or why, when such equilibrium is reached, it should be preserved.

Thus innovations may change the equilibrium share of wages in one direction, but the process of development may change the actual share in the opposite direction. In general, equilibrium analysis will only give us the answers we seek when we can be sure that the process of adjustment is from one equilibrium to another[4] and that is a very large assumption to make when dealing with problems of economic development. If this assumption cannot be made then there is no process of adjustment in the strict sense and the only way of analysis is to follow the variable we are interested in from one period to the next.

In the previous chapter we have already laid down certain general guiding principles in this sort of analysis. In particular we explained the importance which attaches to the investment ratio in determining the *ex post* share of wages. We may here extend our analysis in the following way.

Given any stream of innovations and given the rate of population growth there will be, at any one moment of time, one particular level and rate of growth of income which may be called the equilibrium rate of growth (y_e) and the equilibrium level of income (Y_e). It will be clear from our previous work that y_e and Y_e are only points of reference and that there is no *a priori* reason why they should ever be established. But given y_e and Y_e there will also be an equilibrium path of the share of wages, that is to say there will be one share of wages at each moment of time at which producers, expanding output at the equilibrium rate, have maximised their profits (utility), (and are in long run equilibrium) and at which the proportion of income demanded in the form of consumption goods is equal to the proportion of income supplied in the form of these goods.

Now the actual rate of growth of income (y) may at some times exceed y_e and sometimes fall short of it. But the trend rate of growth of income (y_t) may equal the equilibrium rate of growth of income. We may also define a trend, or average level of income (Y_t) and the latter may be above, equal to, or below the equilibrium level of income Y_e. Now, as we saw in our discussion of the trade cycle, the share of wages will tend to be below its equilibrium values when $y > y_e$ and above its equilibrium value when $y < y_e$. If now $Y_t > Y_e$ then this implies that on the average $y > y_e$ more frequently than $y < y_e$. Hence there is a presumption that on the average the share of wages is more frequently below its equilibrium value than above it, so that the trend share of wages will tend to lie below its equilibrium value. The reverse will tend to be the case when $Y_t < Y_e$.

Before we proceed any further we must note that this approach can at best only be a rough guide to the problem at hand and that no great precision is claimed for it. All we wish to say is that there is a presumption (but not a certainty) that a trend level of income higher than the equilibrium level will tend to lower the path of the trend share of wages below its equilibrium path and vice versa for $Y_t < Y_e$. This presumption is based on the fact that when $y > y_e$ the investment ratio will be above its equilibrium value and when $y < y_e$ it will be below its equilibrium value. But we cannot be certain that for instance $Y_t = Y_e$ implies that the trend share of wages will equal its equilibrium value. This depends on the degree of price flexibility and a host of other things.

This much being understood we can carry our analysis a step further. If the excess of Y_t over Y_e is growing through time, that is if $y_t > y_e$ then the trend share of wages may diminish while the equilibrium share is increasing. There is no reason why this should not occur. Periods of rapid growth and development are frequently also periods of high positive abnormal profits. In times of rapid innovations and population growth, periods of booms and prosperity will be longer and more marked than periods of depression, hence while the equilibrium level and rate of growth may be increasing, the trend level and rate of growth may be increasing even more rapidly. I think that there can be little doubt that in such periods the equilibrium and trend share of wages may be moving in opposite directions. How far such a divergent movement may go depends on a large number of factors. There is no guarantee that the traditional static stabilising forces will perform the same function in a dynamic set-up. Thus in a static analysis, if the share of wages is below its equilibrium value, producers will expand output until prices have fallen and equilibrium is established. In a dynamic analysis, the impetus to expansion given by the divergence may be destabilising, since it may mean an even greater desire to invest and thus perhaps a further increase in the divergence between Y_t and Y_e.

Exactly the same type of analysis can be applied to the case where the excess of Y_e over Y_t is increasing, i.e. $y_e > y_t$. Here it is possible for the trend share of wages to increase while the equilibrium share is diminishing. This will be a period of relative stagnation and negative abnormal profits will be more frequent. Again there is no guarantee that there will be any automatic forces to reduce the divergence between Y_e and Y_t.

We may therefore lay down the following very general and rough principles.

1 If $y_t = y_e$ then the trend path of the share of wages will tend to lie below or above the equilibrium path accordingly as $Y_t > Y_e$ or $Y_t < Y_e$.

2 If $y_t \gtrless y_e$ there is a possibility that the equilibrium and trend path of the share of wages may diverge.

3 Therefore secular movements in the share of wages are determined

as much by the process of development and adjustment to new situations as by changes in the equilibrium share of wages. Because of this it is not profitable to attempt to lay down precise principles concerning secular movements in the share of wages since the process of adjustment varies with the type of innovations undertaken, with population growth, with monetary policy and with countless other factors.

II

If the general approach and conclusions outlined in the previous section are correct then the theories of distribution in the long run, based on the assumption of continued equilibrium, involve not only an enormous simplification of reality but may also lead us to expect certain general directions of change which in fact never materialise. As has been pointed out by Samuelson, a comparative statics approach is only valid if we 1) have a dynamic theory as well and 2) can be sure that the final equilibrium can be reached and is independent of the path of adjustment. There is no reason why, in dealing with long run historical processes, 2) should hold, and in any case the onus of proof that 2) in fact is satisfied rests on those who habitually indulge in a comparative statics approach to long run problems.

It is therefore especially dangerous when writers, on the basis of a highly simplified partial equilibrium theory of distribution, attempt to explain the changes in distribution that have actually taken place. Both Hicks and Kalecki have attempted this, although Hicks, one suspects, never took his brief references to this problem very seriously.

As we saw in chapter 10, Hicks analysed the effect of innovations on the share of wages by means of the elasticity of substitution (σ). Thus he maintained that if $\sigma = 1$, innovations will leave the share of wages unaffected. Since such statistics as there are seemed to exhibit a remarkable constancy in the share of wages over long periods, Hicks concluded that the elasticity of substitution must in fact have been equal to unity.[5]

But this of course does not follow. For one thing the elasticity of substitution is not the only determinant of the distribution of income; profit margins and the price of raw materials will also have to be taken into account. But quite apart from this, a given event can only be explained by a particular theory if all the events postulated by the theory actually occurred. Thus in order to show that it was a unit elasticity of substitution that kept the share of wages constant Hicks would have to show:

1 that all production functions were of such a form as to lead to $\sigma = 1$.

2 that producers at all times produced every output at minimum unit cost, i.e. that the ratio of the marginal products of any two factors equalled the ratio of their prices (marginal costs). Failing that, that divergences from this minimum cost equilibrium were small.
3 that profit margins or what we have called the 'exploitation coefficient' remained constant throughout.
4 that raw material prices either did not vary or, if they did vary, that raw materials were also subject to substitution and that the elasticity of substitution between raw materials and any other factor was also equal to unity.

Hicks showed none of these things and we must therefore conclude that at the very best his explanation of the constancy in the share of wages is unproven. We cannot of course say that it is wrong, since a unit elasticity of substitution is, under certain assumptions, one of the possible causes of a constant share of wages, and whether or not these assumptions are fulfilled is a question of fact and not of theory.

Kalecki carried his attempt to explain the alleged constancy of the share of wages in the long run much further than Hicks. We have already examined Kalecki's theory of distribution in some detail in a previous chapter. On the basis of this theory Kalecki explains the constancy of the share of wages over the long run by equal but opposite secular movements in the degree of monopoly and the ratio of raw material costs to total prime costs, the former according to Kalecki having increased and the latter diminished.[6]

Now as far as the facts are concerned, Rostow[7] has recently shown that for the period 1880–1913:
1 the short period marginal cost curve was not constant,
2 these short period costs were not uniquely relevant to price formation and
3 the competitive position of British industry in the period 1873–1900 actually increased and that the subsequent decline in the intensity of competition was not due to an increase in institutional monopoly.

It has also been pointed out by Dunlop that Kalecki's explanation of the constancy of the share of wages ignores changes in the structure of the economy. For if this structure changes, then even though the degree of monopoly in each industry remains constant, the average degree of monopoly will change. But there have clearly been many changes in the structure of the economy in the period under consideration, so that an increase in the degree of monopoly in some industries may still be consistent with a fall in the average degree of monopoly. In fact it has been shown that those industries in which there was a presumption that the degree of monopoly increased also declined in relative importance.[8]

So much for the facts. If Rostow is correct, neither Kalecki's assertions of facts nor their explanations are valid. But quite apart from the empirical foundation of Kalecki's analysis, there is the following theoretical objection to it. The degree of monopoly is only measured *ex post* by Kalecki by examining the gross profit margin. But the latter is only equal to the former in equilibrium, i.e. when *ex ante* supply equals *ex ante* demand. There is no reason why, at the dates when gross profit margin data are collected, this condition should be satisfied, especially if the period is one of considerable change and adjustment.

When Kalecki says that the degree of monopoly has increased he therefore really means that the gross profit margin has increased, in which case his explanation of a constant share of wages is a mere arithmetical truism. The degree of monopoly as used in Kalecki's theory is an *ex ante* concept and a property of the *ex ante* demand curves facing producers. As already noted elsewhere it has nothing whatever to do with, say, the degree of concentration of an industry or the distribution of the ownership of the means of production, for which presumably some measure could be found.[9] Unless Kalecki can take the important step and show that producers on the average were always in equilibrium, his explanation of the constancy of the share of wages must be taken as unproven.

Not only are the explanations of a constant share of wages inadequate, but the constancy of the share in actual fact is not beyond dispute. Thus Rostow shows that in the period 1880–1913 for Great Britain

> 'the course of events yielded almost certainly a modest favourable shift in the distribution of income for labour until about 1900 and an unfavourable shift from that time to 1913'.[10]

Given the paucity of the statistical material, this cannot be taken as a final verdict, but neither on the other hand can the constancy of the share of wages be regarded as proven beyond reasonable doubt.

III

What then is the outcome of the discussion of this chapter? We hope to have demonstrated the theoretical possibility at least of the actual share of wages moving in the opposite direction to the equilibrium share. Because of this and other shortcomings we have rejected the long run theories and explanations of observed phenomena based on the assumption that the economy is typically in equilibrium. That assumption is in glaring contrast to the discussions, sometimes found in the same volume in which these equilibrium theories are propounded, of the trade cycle which is regarded as a permanent phenomenon.

But beyond criticising these theories we have been unable to offer a simple alternative. The real world is enormously complex and the wider our time-horizon the more difficult it becomes to compress everything into a simple formula. We have tentatively suggested that in times of rapid expansion, when the rate of innovation and obsolescence is high and population is growing, the share of wages is likely to experience a secular decline owing to the tendency for the investment ratio to be more or less permanently above its equilibrium value. For similar reasons we have tentatively suggested that in times of relative stagnation the reverse would be true. But this hunch is as unproven as are the theories we have been criticising and not too much reliance can be placed on it.

In particular it must be remembered that we have been exclusively concerned with a closed economy. Once this restriction is relaxed, the ratio of consumption goods to total output is not only determined by domestic production but also by the volume of imports. Favourable and unfavourable shifts in the terms of trade, the proportion of income exported, gold movements etc. will all influence the ratio of consumption goods to output and it is quite impossible to take these variables as given in a long run analysis.

Conclusions

In this book we have broadly attempted two things: 1) to state the theory of distribution in macro-economic terms and 2) to explore the implications of disequilibrium and dynamic adjustments.

1 The theory of distribution currently held by most economists has not altered significantly since the publication of Marshall's *Principles.* This theory, as we have noted, is derived from the assumption that individual firms maximise their money profit. Such changes as have taken place in this analysis are either in the nature of refinements (the elasticity of substitution) or due to the abandonment of the perfect competition assumption. The only significant departure from the main trend of thought is Kalecki's analysis of the degree of monopoly. This we decided to treat as a special case applying only to depression equilibrium.

As long as entrepreneurs can be assumed to maximise their money profits, the partial Marshallian analysis is beyond reproach. This assumption is however unnecessarily restrictive and out of line with the present theory of individual choice. We therefore substituted the maximisation of utility (index of utility) for the maximisation of money profit. In a partial analysis this, beyond introducing a subjective element into an otherwise objective and mechanical analysis, and defining explicitly a supply curve of entrepreneurship, makes little difference to the main results. But in a macro-economic model it is of some significance.

The transition from a partial to a general analysis of distribution has hardly ever been explicitly examined. To have shown how the income of an individual firm was distributed between the various participants in production was regarded as sufficient. But some of the variables which enter into a general equilibrium analysis are not independent of the distribution of income. The general analysis will therefore impose additional constraints on the equilibrium distribution of income which are not taken into account by the partial model.

The short period macro-economic model of chapters 3 to 5 was based on the Keynesian assumption that the propensity to consume is an increasing function of the share of wages. We also postulated that the supply curve of 'entrepreneurship' was less than perfectly elastic at a given marginal profit. Making certain simplifying assumptions we showed that the equilibrium share of wages would be that share at which the output produced when producers have maximised their utility is equal to the output demanded. These conditions are of course no more than we would expect, although the current habit of working exclusively in real terms has led to the neglect of the factors determining the supply of output.

The (static) stability conditions of our model were however more interesting. We found for instance that a fall in money wages may lead to a fall in the share of wages even though the elasticity of substitution was greater than unity and the price of capital constant. For in so far as the fall in wages leads to an increase in output and in the demand for capital (investment), the share of wages may be reduced because the equilibrium propensity to consume is reduced. For the same reason a fall in the 'degree of monopoly' may reduce the share of wages. Results such as these cannot be derived from a partial analysis alone and justify our excursion into macro-economics.

Many of these problems were neglected in the past because of the additional assumption that net investment was zero. Once stationary state equilibria are compared, the macro-economic analysis adds little to our understanding of the factors determining the distribution of income, and the partial model is adequate. The assumption of stationary states however is far too restrictive to have permitted us to continue to use it. But the difficulty now arose that as long as net investment is positive (or negative) the stock of capital is changing, so that we cannot remain satisfied with a model which assumes that the stock of capital remains constant. Something analogous to the Marshallian long period analysis was required.

Recent advances in the theory of dynamics enabled us to lay down certain tentative propositions. The analogue to the stationary state is dynamic equilibrium. The conditions for the latter are that the stock of capital should be growing at such a rate as to enable a given rate of growth in output to be produced at the minimum cost factor ratio such that the rate of growth in output in any one period is equal to the rate of growth in demand. In addition of course aggregate demand must equal aggregate supply in each period. Using these conditions we found that in the absence of a certain type and rate of innovations, the equilibrium share of wages would be inversely related to the equilibrium rate of growth of output. The technical difficulties involved in the use of difference equations with variable coefficients prevented us from stating these results rigorously. But sufficient was done to show that a macro-economic analysis of dynamic equilibrium, just as the macro-economic analysis of short run equilibrium, imposed additional constraints on the equilibrium share of wages not taken into account in the partial model. In particular the equilibrium share of wages is that share which is compatible with dynamic equilibrium as defined above, and since the latter is not independent of the share going to labour there is no reason to suppose that any share of wages is compatible with dynamic equilibrium.

2 The conditions of dynamic equilibrium were found to be very restrictive. What is more there was little reason to suppose that such an equilibrium would be stable. The accumulated weight of evidence of economic fluctuations seemed to suggest that in any case dynamic equilibrium in the strict sense is rarely if ever attained. If then anything was to be said about the actual distribution of income at any one moment of time, something more than the equilibrium approach was needed.

We dealt with this problem by assuming flexible prices and making use of the relationship between the propensity to consume and the share of wages. We noted the fact, so constantly stressed by the classicals, that at any one moment of time no more could be consumed than was available. This simple principle has in modern times been greatly obscured partly because much else of what the classicals deduced from this (e.g. their theory of employment) could not be accepted, partly because Keynesian analysis has until very recently assumed that all adjustments were more or less timeless. Recent work in Keynesian dynamics has however rehabilitated the time dimension in economics, and with it at least part of the wage fund doctrine.

In almost all cases we found that the wage fund approach could yield results where the modern approach could not. It enabled us to make at least an attempt at providing some sort of answer to the problem of the effect of innovations on the distribution of income, without having to assume away the process of 'adjustment'. It helped us in analysing the probable course of the share of wages in the course of the trade cycle without having to make the dubious assumption that entrepreneurs are always in equilibrium in the sense that *ex ante* marginal revenue is equal to *ex ante* marginal cost. It even gave us some help in the great problem of secular movements in the share of wages. In all cases in which the orthodox equilibrium approach yielded results, the wage fund approach yielded similar ones. In all cases where the former left us helpless the latter came to our aid.

But we must emphasise yet once again that this does not mean that the Marshallian analysis should be abandoned. We need a proper equilibrium theory before we can hope to tackle the more difficult problems of dynamic adjustments. Nor should the analysis of this book be regarded as more than a first approach. The unfortunate fact is that our tools of dynamic analysis are still in a rudimentary state. Thus for instance we must always assume that all economic relations are linear. We must also frequently regard many propensities as fundamental constants when they clearly are not. There can therefore be no certainty about our conclusions at this stage. What we hope to have done is to indicate certain directions in which the theory of distribution may perhaps be profitably extended.

Notes

Preface

1 Dennis H. Robertson, 'Wage Grumbles', *Economic Fragments,* P.S. King and Son, 1931.

2 Joan Robinson, 'Equilibrium Growth Models', *American Economic Review,* June 1961.

3 C.J. Bliss, 'Rates of Return in a Linear Model', Cambridge, January 1968, mimeographed.

4 Michio Morishima, *Equilibrium, Stability and Growth,* Oxford, 1969.

5 On page 70 I write: '. . . In a regular progressing economy the share of wages will be determined by orthodox factors: the degree of monopoly, the production function and the prices of the factors of production.' This view I still hold although I would not state it in this form. In particular I would avoid the aggregates like 'production function'.

6 N. Kaldor, 'Alternative Theories of Distribution', *Review of Economic Studies,* London Vol. XXIII, No. 2, 1955–6.

7 Joan Robinson, *Essays in the Theory of Economic Growth,* London, Macmillan, 1962, pp. 48 et seq.

8 Good economists always understood this. For instance see the section entitled: 'No valid classification of productive agencies into "factors" is possible' in Frank H. Knight, *Risk, Uncertainty and Profit,* Boston, New York, Houghton Mifflin and Co., 1921.

Introduction

1 *'Entrepreneur faisant ni bénéfice ni perte'* in L. Walras, *Abrégé d'Eléments d'Economie Politique Pure,* P. Richon and R. Durand, Paris, 1953, p. 288. This assumption implies that the supply of entrepreneurs is perfectly elastic at zero profits.

2 As long as we assume perfect competition, Euler's Theorem will hold and profits of entrepreneurs will equal their marginal product. This is of course consistent with a zero profit. If perfect competition is not assumed, then Euler's theorem will only continue to hold when profits are again equal to zero or 'normal'. See Joan Robinson, 'Euler's Theorem and the problem of distribution', *Economic Journal,* XLIV (1934), pp. 398–414. But since 'normal' profits cannot be defined without reference to a supply function of

entrepreneurs this is not very helpful. If Euler's Theorem does not hold then profits are a 'residual' income. For an excellent survey of the 'adding up' problem see G. Stigler, *Production and Distribution Theories,* London, Macmillan, 1946, chapter 12.

3 Joan Robinson, *The Economics of Imperfect Competition,* London, Macmillan, 1945, pp. 92–3. See also R. Triffin's criticism of this concept in *Monopolistic Competition and General Equilibrium Theory,* Harvard, 1947, pp. 135 et seq.

4 This assumption was frequently made by older writers, e.g. 'In trades in which the speculative element is not very important, so that the work of management consists chiefly of superintendance, the earnings of management will follow pretty closely the amount of work done in the business . . . ,' A. Marshall, *Principles of Economics,* 8th edition, London, Macmillan, 1930 pp. 613–4.

5 E.g. A.G. Hart, 'Anticipations, Uncertainty and Dynamic Planning', *Studies in Business Administration,* Vol. XI, No. 1, Chicago, 1940, pp. 25 et seq. Also by the same author: 'Imputation and the Demand for Productive Resources in Disequilibrium', *Explorations in Economics,* New York, McGraw-Hill, 1936, pp. 268 et seq. Also G. Tintner, 'The Theory of Production under non-static conditions', *Journal of Political Economy,* Chicago, Vol. I, No. 5, 1942, pp. 645 et seq.

6 Certain implications of this assumption have been examined by T. de Scitovsky in 'A note on profit maximisation and its implications', *Review of Economic Studies,* Vol. XI, 1943–4, pp. 57–60, and by W. J. Baumol and H. Makower in 'The Analogy between Producer and Consumer Equilibrium Analysis', *Economica,* London, Vol. XVII, 1950, pp. 63–81.

7 See I. Little, *A Critique of Welfare Economics,* Oxford, 1950, pp. 14–37. Also P. Samuelson, 'Consumption Theory in terms of Revealed Preferences', *Economica,* November 1948.

8 P. Samuelson, *Foundations of Economic Analysis,* Harvard, 1947, pp. 113–16.

9 This has been examined by a number of writers, in particular G. Stigler, 'Production and Distribution in the short run', *Journal of Political Economy,* Vol. 49, 1939, pp. 305–27.

10 E.g. Mr R.F. Harrod's use of a 'warranted' (in equilibrium) rate of growth of output in his *Towards a Dynamic Economics,* London, Macmillan, 1948, Chapter 3. Also E. Domar, 'Capital Expansion, Rate of Growth and Employment', *Econometrica,* New Haven Conn.,

1946. Recently the concept has been re-examined by J.R. Hicks, *A Contribution to the Theory of the Trade Cycle,* Oxford, 1950, chapter 5 and elsewhere in the book.

11 P. Samuelson, *Foundations,* op. cit., pp. 78–9.

Chapter 1

1 This is what Professor Samuelson has called the 'Correspondence Principle'. See P. Samuelson, *Foundations,* op. cit. p. 258 et seq.

2 The term was first invented by Hicks. See J.R. Hicks, *The Theory of Wages,* London, Macmillan, 1932. Hicks' use of this measure led to an extensive discussion. The main participants in the discussion were: J. Robinson, *The Economics of Imperfect Competition* op. cit, notes on the elasticity of substitution by P.M. Sweezy, A.P. Lerner, R.F. Kahn, *Review of Economic Studies,* 1933; further notes by L. Tarshis, A.P. Lerner, J.E. Meade, *Review of Economic Studies,* 1934; and yet further notes by F. Machlup, A.P. Lerner, J. Robinson and M. Friedman in the *Review of Economic Studies,* 1935. Also 'The Elasticity of Substitution' by A.C. Pigou, *Economic Journal,* London, June 1934, and notes by R.F. Kahn and D.G. Champernowne in the *Economic Journal,* June 1935. Lastly J.R. Hicks, 'Distribution and Economic Progress: A Revised Version', *Review of Economic Studies,* 1936.

3 J.R. Hicks, *Theory of Wages,* London, op. cit., p. 255.

4 J. Robinson, *Economics of Imperfect Competition,* op. cit., p. 256.

5 D.G. Champernowne, op. cit.

6 Let $\frac{F_a}{F_b} = z$, then Robinson's formula for the elasticity of substitution can be rewritten after evaluating $d\left(\frac{b}{a}\right)$ as

$$\sigma = \frac{z}{ab} \; \frac{az + b}{z\,\frac{\partial z}{\partial b} - \frac{\partial z}{\partial a}} \, . \qquad (6.1)$$

Evaluating $\frac{\partial z}{\partial a}$ and $\frac{\partial z}{\partial b}$ we have

$$\sigma = \frac{F_a\, F_b\, (aF_a + bF_b)}{ab\,(F_{aa}\, F_b^2 - 2\, F_{ab}\, F_a\, F_b + F_{bb}\, F_a^2} \, . \qquad (6.2)$$

In the special case of constant returns to scale by Euler's Theorem

$$F_{aa} = \frac{-b}{a} F_{ab}; \quad F_{bb} = \frac{-a}{b} F_{ab}. \qquad (6.3)$$

Substituting in 6.2 and rearranging we find

$$\sigma = \frac{F_a F_b}{x F_{ab}}, \qquad (6.4)$$

which is Hicks' formula for the elasticity of substitution.

7 We have three equilibrium conditions when there are only two factors of production:

$$x = F(a, b,) = f(\pi) \qquad (7.1)$$

where $f(\pi)$ is the demand function for the product and 7.1 states that demand must equal supply;

$$\pi F_a = w^a \qquad (7.2)$$

$$\pi F_b = w^b. \qquad (7.3)$$

These two conditions simply state that the wage of the factors A and B must equal their marginal value product. Partially differentiating 7.1, 7.2 and 7.3 with respect to w^a, and assuming constant returns to scale we obtain three equations in the three unknowns, $\frac{\partial \pi}{\partial a}$, $\frac{\partial a}{\partial w^a}$, $\frac{\partial b}{\partial w^a}$ thus

$$xe \frac{\partial \pi}{\partial a} + w^a \frac{\partial a}{\partial w^a} + w^b \frac{\partial b}{\partial w^a} = 0 \qquad (7.4)$$

$$x\sigma \frac{\partial \pi}{\partial a} - \frac{b}{a} w^b \frac{\partial a}{\partial w^a} + w^b \frac{\partial b}{\partial w^a} = \frac{x\pi}{w^a} \sigma \qquad (7.5)$$

$$x\sigma \frac{\partial \pi}{\partial a} + w^b \frac{\partial a}{\partial w^a} - \frac{a}{b} w^a \frac{\partial b}{\partial w^a} = 0. \qquad (7.6)$$

From this it is easy to find that

$$\frac{\partial b}{\partial w^a} = \frac{-ab}{x\pi}(e - \sigma) \qquad (7.7)$$

so that

$$\epsilon = \frac{\partial b}{\partial w^a}\frac{w^a}{b} = -\frac{W^a}{x}(e - \sigma). \qquad (7.8)$$

It follows that if $e = \sigma$, $\epsilon = 0$, and the demand for B will be unaffected by the change in w^a. When $e > \sigma$, then $\epsilon < 0$ and hence the demand for B will increase when w^a falls, and diminish when w^a increases, and vice versa when $\epsilon > 0$. This is Robinson's well known theorem. See J. Robinson, *Economics of Imperfect Competition,* op. cit., p. 259.

8 R.F. Kahn, *Review of Economic Studies,* 1933, and J.R. Hicks, 'Distribution and Economic Progress: A Revised Version', *Review of Economic Studies,* 1936.

9 Strictly speaking we should use arc elasticities and not point elasticities.

10 J.R. Hicks, 'Distribution and Economic Progress', op. cit.

11 Joan Robinson, *Review of Economic Studies,* 1935, p. 149.

12 Mr. Kahn using the 'real elasticity of demand' naturally concluded that since the latter is infinitely great $e > \sigma$ always, so that the backward sloping supply curve of B could not upset the normal conditions for a change in A's share when w^a changed.

13 P. Samuelson, *Foundations,* op. cit., p. 7.

Chapter 2

1 M. Kalecki, 'Costs and Prices', *Studies in Economic Dynamics,* London, George Allen and Unwin, 1943. Also 'The Distribution of the National Income', *Essays in the Theory of Economic Fluctuations,* London, George Allen and Unwin, 1939.

2 M. Kalecki, 'Costs and Prices', p. 10.

3 M. Kalecki, 'Costs and Prices', p. 12.

4 L. Reynolds, 'Relation between Wage Rates, Costs and Prices', *American Economic Review, Supplement,* 1942. See also W. J. Eiteman, 'Factors Determining the Location of the Least Cost Point', *American Economic Review,* December 1948, pp. 98–109,

and H. Apel, 'Marginal Cost Constancy and its Implications', *American Economic Review,* December 1948, pp. 870–85.

5 M. Kalecki, *Essays in the Theory of Economic Fluctuations,* loc. cit.

6 'We should all argue that if we start from a level of output very greatly below capacity, so that even the most efficient plant and labour are only partially employed, marginal real cost may be expected to decline with increasing output, or, at the worst, remain constant. But a point must surely come long before plant and labour are fully employed . . . Even if one concedes that the course of the short-period marginal cost curve is downwards in its early reaches, Mr Kahn's assumption that it eventually turns upwards is on general common sense grounds surely beyond reasonable question, and that this happens moreover on a part of the curve which is highly relevant for practical purposes.'

J.M. Keynes, 'Relative Movements of Real Wages and Output', *Economic Journal,* 1939, pp. 44–5.

7 The question of what is meant by 'divisibility' and its role in determining the shape of the cost curve is controversial. Here we shall only wish to mean by divisibility of capital or equipment, that it is possible to alter the amount of equipment by relatively small (if finite) amounts. See also E.H. Chamberlin, 'Proportionality, Divisibility, and Economies of Scale', *Quarterly Journal of Economics,* Cambridge, Mass., February 1948, pp. 229–62.

8 N. Kaldor, 'The Equilibrium of the Firm', *Economic Journal,* 1934.

9 S.C. Tsiang, *The Variations of Real Wages and Profit Margins in relation to the Trade Cycle,* London, Pitman, 1947, p. 61.

10 A.P. Lerner, 'The Concept of Monopoly and the Measurement of Monopoly Power', *Review of Economic Studies,* 1934.

11 E.H. Chamberlin, *The Theory of Monopolistic Competition,* Harvard, 1947.

Chapter 3

1 For a full analysis see P. Samuelson, *Foundations,* pp. 107–16.

2 I am thus supposing the marginal utility of income to be constant.

3 P. Samuelson, 'Constancy of the Marginal Utility of Income', *Studies in Mathematical Economics and Econometrics, In Honour of Henry Schultz,* Chicago, University of Chicago, 1942, pp. 75–91.

4 The increase in total profit (marginal profit) is equal to the difference between marginal revenue and marginal cost. This by a well known formula can be written as

$$\frac{\partial P}{\partial x} = \pi\left(1 - \frac{1}{e}\right) - c\left(1 + \frac{1}{\epsilon}\right) \quad (4.1)$$

where π is price, e the elasticity of demand, c is average cost and ϵ the elasticity of the cost curve. If now there is an iso-elastic shift in the demand curve as defined in the text, then at the same π marginal profits will be the same as before; for we are assuming $c(1 + 1/\epsilon)$ constant. Further, at the same π, P/x the profit per unit of output will be the same as before. Hence the relationship between average and marginal profit remains constant. If we like we can say that an iso-elastic (horizontally) shift in the demand curve causes an iso-elastic (horizontally) shift in the profit curve.

5 This follows from 4. For the slope of a line through the origin measures average profit. The slope of OP measures marginal profit. Hence, since the shift in the demand curve leaves the relationship between average and marginal profit unchanged, the OP curves must have the same slopes along a line through the origin.

6 For a producer producing under constant costs and faced with a downwards sloping demand curve, average profits will be falling with output. Hence given our assumptions concerning the shifts in the demand curve, the higher the average profit the higher the marginal profit. But the higher the marginal profit (the steeper the slope of OP) the further to the right will be the tangency of OP and any indifference curve, i.e. the greater will be output. And since the relation between average and marginal profit is assumed constant we can simply say that output will be an increasing function of average profit.

7 See J.S. Duesenberry, *Income, Saving, and the Theory of Consumer Behaviour,* Harvard, 1949.

8 It may be thought that the subsistence wage not only depends on the share of wages but also on the absolute level of income. This, however, is not so. For if at any value $(W/X) = (W/X)_0$ and $X = X_0$ wage earners are at subsistence, then an increase in X to $X_1 > X_0$ at the same share of wages will mean that employment has increased in the same proportion as X. For we are assuming constant returns. Whether or not workers are at subsistence depends therefore only on (W/X) and not on X.

9 Since our analysis is one of short period flow equilibrium, i.e. we assume the stock of capital constant, the supply curve is reversible when output exceeds equilibrium output. We must assume that

investment orders get cancelled as prices fall.

10 A constant marginal disutility of producing implies that the indifference curves of the entrepreneur are straight lines, i.e. have constant slopes. Thus the equilibrium slope of the profit transformation curve OP (marginal profit) must be constant for all outputs since in equilibrium the latter curve is tangential to an indifference curve. We have already seen that on our assumptions a constant marginal profit implies a constant average profit. Therefore the supply curve is perfectly elastic with respect to average profits.

Chapter 4

1 See J. T. Dunlop, *Wage Determination under Trade Unions,* second edition, Oxford, Blackwell, 1950, pp. 163 et seq.

2 See D. Patinkin, 'Relative Prices, Say's Law and the Demand for Money', *Econometrica,* 1948. We can get over these difficulties by postulating a perfectly (interest) elastic supply of money.

Chapter 5

1 Hitch and Hall, 'Price Theory and Business Behaviour', *Oxford Economic Papers,* May 1939.

2 Kalecki commenting on the full cost principle relates this experience: 'In a modern cotton spinning mill the manager described once to me at great length the work of their calculating department. To my question however, how the results are used to fix prices, he replied: "Oh the prices are fixed by the market" ', *Studies in Economic Dynamics,* op. cit., p. 27.

3 See Tsiang, *The Variations of Real Wages and Profit Margins,* op. cit.

Chapter 6

1 See Kalecki, 'Principle of Increasing Risk', in *Essays in the Theory of Economic Fluctuations,* op. cit., pp. 98–102.

2 This increase in uncertainty will not only be reflected in a higher marginal rate of profit, but also in a rising marginal cost of borrowing.

3 It should be noted that since we assumed a given level of income to start with, in Chapter 3, the above considerations do not invalidate our conclusions given there. On the other hand, of course, since our treatment was concerned with short period flow equilibrium, it could not take explicit account of rates of growth of output.

4 J.R. Hicks, *A Contribution to the Theory of the Trade Cycle,* op. cit., Chapter 5, and mathematical appendix, sections 17, 18 and 29.

5 In equilibrium stocks neither accumulate nor decumulate.

6 This can be easily shown as follows. We know that

$$\Delta Y_t = \alpha I_{t-1} . \qquad (6.1)$$

Let the equilibrium rate of growth in income, $\dfrac{\Delta Y_t}{Y_{t-1}} = g$

whence $\Delta Y_t = gY_{t-1}$. Substituting in 6.1 we have

$$\frac{gY_{t-1}}{I_{t-1}} = \alpha . \qquad (6.2)$$

If α is constant, then if g increases Y_{t-1}/I_{t-1} must diminish, i.e. the ratio of investment to income must increase.

7 We have

$${}_1\lambda = \sqrt{\alpha v} = {}_1\gamma = \frac{(c+v) + \sqrt{(c+v)^2 - 4v}}{2} \qquad (7.1)$$

Let $(c + v) = R$. Then

$$(2\sqrt{\alpha v} - R)^2 - R^2 - 4v. \qquad (7.2)$$

Expanding and eliminating we have

$$(\alpha v + v)^2 = \alpha v R^2 .$$

Therefore

$$-v + \sqrt{\frac{(\alpha v + v)^2}{\alpha v}} = c. \qquad (7.3)$$

8 If we differentiate 6.11 with respect to v we have

$$\frac{\partial}{\partial v}\left[-v + \sqrt{\frac{(\alpha v + v)^2}{\alpha v}}\right] = -1 + \frac{1}{2}\left[\frac{(\alpha v + v)^2}{\alpha v}\right]^{-\frac{1}{2}}$$

$$\times \left[\frac{\alpha v 2(\alpha v + v)(\alpha + 1) - \alpha(\alpha v + v)^2}{(\alpha v)^2}\right] \qquad (8.1)$$

which can be reduced to

$$-1 + \frac{1}{2}\left[\frac{(\alpha v + v)^2}{\alpha v}\right]^{-\frac{1}{2}}\left[\frac{(\alpha + 1)^2}{\alpha}\right]. \qquad (8.2)$$

Now 8.2 will be < 0 when

$$v > \frac{(\alpha + 1)^2}{4\alpha} \qquad (\alpha > 1) \qquad (8.3)$$

Since the right-hand part of 8.3 is always less than α, the expression 8.1 will always be negative as long as the roots of the equations in the text remain positive and real. Hence an increase in v diminishes the equilibrium value of c and, *ceteris paribus*, of W/Y.

9 Whether W/Y diminishes or increases with α depends on the effect of the latter on v.

10 It should be noted that we have assumed that all the roots of our equations are real. This need not be so, and if we neglect autonomous investment, the only possible equilibrium income may be zero. When autonomous investment is included everything is greatly simplified. For the equilibrium income must be growing at the same rate as autonomous investment is growing if *ex ante* investment is to equal *ex ante* saving. If then we are correct in assuming that in the absence of innovations the ratio of investment to output is an increasing function of the equilibrium rate of growth, the *ex ante* propensity to consume must always diminish when the rate of growth of autonomous investment is increased.

Chapter 7

1 E.g. F.W. Taussig, *Wages and Capital*, London, Macmillan, 1896, and G. Stigler, *Production and Distribution Theories*, New York, Macmillan, 1946.

2 I.e. by the 'coefficient of exploitation', see chapter 4.

3 Assuming that capitalists consume nothing and that there is no consumption lag. These assumptions are *not* necessary to the analysis and are only made for the sake of simplicity.

4 Our basic equation would then read

$$C_t^s = C_{t-1}^s + m(C_{t-1}^d - C_{t-1}^s) + n(C_{t-1}^d - C_{t-2}^d).$$

In terms of proportions of income this becomes:

$$\left(\frac{W}{Y}\right)_t = \mu_1 \left(\frac{W}{Y}\right)_{t-1} + m\mu_1 \left[\left(\frac{W}{Y}\right)_e - \left(\frac{W}{Y}\right)_{t-1}\right] + n \left[\mu_1 \left(\frac{W}{Y}\right)_e - \mu_2 \left(\frac{W}{Y}\right)_e\right]$$

where $\mu_2 = Y_{t-2}/Y_t$. From this we find:

$$\left(\frac{\overline{W}}{Y}\right) = \frac{\left(\frac{W}{Y}\right)_e (m\mu_1 + n\mu_1 - n\mu_2)}{1 - \mu_1 + m\mu_1}$$

Since $\mu_2 < \mu_1$, $(1 - \mu_1) > 0$ when $\left(\frac{\overline{W}}{Y}\right) = \left(\frac{W}{Y}\right)_e$ i.e. $\mu_1 < 1$.

Chapter 8

1 Tsiang, *The Variations of Real Wages and Profit Margins,* op. cit., chapter 2.

2 It should be noted that the current theory of the accelerator implicitly assumes the absence of excess capacity.

3 R.F. Harrod, *The Trade Cycle,* Oxford, The Clarendon Press, 1950.

4 Joan Robinson, review of R.F. Harrod, *The Trade Cycle, Economic Journal,* December 1936.

5 A. Marshall: *Official Papers,* London, Macmillan, 1926. Evidence to Royal Commission on the Depression of Trade and Industry, 1886, p. 8.

6 L. Tarshis, 'Changes in Real and Money Wages', *Economic Journal,* 1939; 'Real Wages in the United States and Great Britain', *Canadian Journal of Economics,* August 1938. Also J.T. Dunlop, 'The Movement of Real and Money Wage Rates', *Economic Journal,* September 1938.

7 S. Tsiang, *Variations of Real Wages and Profit Margins,* op. cit., p. 56.

8 In *Price Flexibility and Employment.*

9 Tsiang, *The Variations of Real Wages and Profit Margins,* op. cit., p. 67

10 See J.T. Dunlop, *Wage Determination under Trade Unions,* Oxford, Blackwell, 1950, chapter 8.

11 Dunlop, *Wage Determination under Trade Unions,* op. cit., chapter 8.

12 Dunlop, *Wage Determination under Trade Unions,* op. cit., p. 163.
13 Dunlop, *Wage Determination under Trade Unions,* op. cit., p. 165.
14 Tsiang, *The Variations of Real Wages and Profit Margins,* op. cit., p. 56.
15 Tsiang, *The Variations of Real Wages and Profit Margins,* op. cit., p. 67.
16 Tsiang, *The Variations of Real Wages and Profit Margins,* op. cit., chapter 6.

Chapter 9

1 J.R. Hicks, *A Contribution to the Theory of the Trade Cycle,* op. cit.
2 Hicks, *A Contribution to the Theory of the Trade Cycle,* op. cit., p. 53.
3 Hicks, *A Contribution to the Theory of the Trade Cycle,* op. cit., p. 39.
4 Hicks, *A Contribution to the Theory of the Trade Cycle,* op. cit., p. 39, note.
5 This, as we shall see, need not be so if we drop the assumption of constant prices. But I cannot see how Hicks reconciles this assumption that the accelerator is zero whenever there is excess capacity, with the further assumption that producers are producing below capacity during the expansion when the accelerator is constant and positive. In the way in which we shall restate the problem presently the output that can be produced when the investment is made is always greater than the output (at non-optimum factor ratio) which induced the investment, but producers will be assumed always to produce at full capacity.
6 Assuming constant returns to scale, ϵ of the previous chapter is equal to unity in long run equilibrium. If $\frac{\Delta Y_t^o}{\Delta Y_t} < 1$ this implies that producers are on their short run cost curves and here $\epsilon > 1$, i.e. W/Y is below its equilibrium value. Moreover, since the above ratio is falling, producers will be producing ever higher up on their short run cost curves and this will normally mean that ϵ will be increasing and therefore W/Y diminishing.
7 See equation 8.5 of chapter 8.
8 Hicks, *A Contribution to the Theory of the Trade Cycle,* op. cit., p. 36, note.
9 Hicks, *A Contribution to the Theory of the Trade Cycle,* op. cit.,

p. 54 et. seq.

10 This is discussed in the next section.

11 For in boom equilibrium we have

$$\left(\frac{C}{Y}\right) = \frac{cE(1+g)^{t-1}}{E(1+g)^t} = \frac{c}{1+g}$$

12 In this section, the share of wages must be taken to mean the share of wages in terms of consumption goods.

13 The following are some general qualifications which must be taken into account.

1 W/Y will change when the structure of production changes. Since during the boom the ratio of investment exceeds, and in the slump falls short of, its equilibrium value, W/Y may exceed its equilibrium value in the boom and fall short of it in the slump, if the share of wages (in terms of its own products) in the investment goods industries greatly exceeds the share of wages in the consumption goods industries.

2 Even though the share of wages in gross or net income produced may fluctuate in the manner indicated in our general analysis, the share of wages in 'income paid out' may remain constant. We have already noted this in the previous chapter.

Chapter 10

1 D. Ricardo, *Political Economy and Taxation,* London, Everyman edition, 1911, p. 263.

2 Ricardo, *Political Economy and Taxation,* op. cit. p. 263.

3 Ricardo, *Political Economy and Taxation,* op. cit. p. 264.

4 Ricardo, *Political Economy and Taxation,* op. cit., p. 267.

5 There is a certain obscurity in Ricardo's writings concerning the factors determining the division of K into C_1 and C_2. It appears however that Ricardo regarded the ratio of C_1 to C_2 as determined by the wage rate. The latter however is itself determined by the quantity of C_2 in existence. To get a determinate solution an equation of the productivity of C_1 must be introduced in showing the relationship between an increase in fixed capital and the rate of interest. For our purposes we can however regard both the wage and interest rate as fixed. For Wicksell's interpretation of what Ricardo meant in this matter see *Finanztheoretische Untersuchungen,* Jena 1896, pp. 23–7, and Stigler, *Production and Distribution Theories,*

op. cit., pp. 284–5.

6 Wicksell, *Lectures on Political Economy,* Vol. 1, London School of Economics Reprints, Routledge, 1938.

7 The mathematics of Wicksell's argument is as follows. Let x and y be the number of labourers per acre before and after the invention. Let f(x) and ϕ(y) be the corresponding production functions. Let m and n be the number of acres used by the first and second method respectively and let B be the total of land available and A the total labour force. We want to find conditions under which

$$mf(x) + n\phi(y) = \max, \qquad (7.1)$$

subject to the two constraints:

$$m + n = B, \qquad (7.2)$$

$$mx = ny = A. \qquad (7.3)$$

Equations 7.2 and 7.3 ensure the full employment of resources. This is a simple maximum problem which yields the conditions

$$f'(x) = \phi'(y), \qquad (7.4)$$

and $$f(x) - xf'(x) = \phi(y) - y\phi'(y). \qquad (7.5)$$

The conditions therefore are that the marginal product of labour 7.4 and of land 7.5 should be equal in both uses when all labour is employed. But this is assumed by free competition. Therefore total product is always maximised under free competition and this must by definition be larger with than without the innovation. Wicksell, op. cit, Vol. I, p. 140.

8 Wicksell, *Lectures on Political Economy,* op. cit.

9 Wicksell, *Lectures on Political Economy,* op. cit.

10 Wicksell, *Lectures on Political Economy,* op. cit.

11 A. Hansen, 'Institutional Friction and Technological Unemployment', *Quarterly Journal of Economics,* 1930–1. 'The Theory of technological progress and the dislocation of employment', *American Economic Review,* 1932. Hansen has of course expressed his views on innovations and their effect on employment frequently since the publication of the above two articles. But it is his earlier theory which

interests us in this historical survey. Some of his later views will be mentioned in the next chapter.

12 A. Hansen, 'Institutional Friction and Technological Unemployment', op. cit.

13 N. Kaldor, 'A case against technical progress', *Economica,* 1932.

14 A. Hansen, 'Institutional friction and Technological Unemployment', op. cit.

15 Professor Haberler in a reply to Hansen (*Quarterly Journal of Economics,* 1931–2) points out that there will be an increase in total money demand for commodities even if there is no change in money wages. This, as shown in the text, is clearly acknowledged by Hansen, and Haberler seems more concerned with a point of exposition than of substance. His assertion that the fall in the number of transactions due to the invention will increase purchasing power and thus lead to a reabsorption of labour is answered by Hansen who points out that once labour is reabsorbed the number of transactions will be the same as before the invention and therefore labour cannot be permanently reabsorbed.

16 N. Kaldor, 'A case against technical progress', op. cit.

17 For a detailed analysis of the effect of a fall in money wages on the level of employment see: O. Lange, *Price Flexibility and Employment,* Principia Press, Bloomington, Indiana, 1944.

18 It is of course well known that Kaldor's views have changed since then and that he does not now regard falling money wages as sufficient to reabsorb the unemployed. See N. Kaldor, 'Professor Pigou on money wages in relation to unemployment', *Economic Journal,* XLVII, 1937, pp. 745–53, and 'Money Wage Cuts in relation to unemployment', *Review of Economic Studies,* VI, 1939, pp. 232–5.

Chapter 11

1 Samuelson has pointed out that all meaningful theorems of comparative statics hinge on stability conditions, and since these must be stated in dynamic form, we must first have a dynamic analysis before comparative statics can be fruitful. He calls this the 'correspondence principle'. Moreover, comparing two equilibrium positions is only possible if there is dynamic stability. See P. Samuelson, *Foundations,* op. cit., pp. 257–83 and p. 324 et seq.

2 If incomes are growing at a constant rate, the stock of capital is also growing at a constant rate. Since there are no innovations, and if factor prices are constant, employment must grow at the same rate

as the stock of capital since the optimum factor ratio is given and constant.

3 By rate of growth in R and K must be understood 'proportionate increase per period'.

4 The rate of growth in R is negative. Hence if the latter is numerically greater than the (positive) rate of growth in K, this implies an elasticity of substitution of less than unity and hence a rise in the share of wages.

5 For various reasons it is better to assume that 'autonomous investment' of Hicks' type, i.e. growing at a constant rate, is not dependent on innovations. For it would force us to assume that innovations are taking place in the downswing and in the depression which seems unlikely. We therefore assume that this type of investment is, say, determined by the government and is unaffected by innovations.

6 The method of analysis here used of comparing two complete systems, identical in all respects except that there is an innovation in one and not in the other, is similar to that used by Kalecki in his 'A Theorem on Technical Progress', *Review of Economic Studies*, Vol. VIII, 1941, pp. 178–84.

7 See chapter 9.

8 Given the propensity to consume, i.e. given a constant share of wages, then since investment, other than autonomous investment, is a function of the rate of growth of output, then the greater the latter, the greater will be the amount invested each period. Also if g is the rate of growth (assumed constant) then the investment ratio is proportional to $g/(1 + g)^2$, assuming a two period lag. The differential of this ratio with respect to g will be positive whenever $1/g > 1$, and this must always be true as long as the rate of growth is less than a hundred per cent. Therefore the ratio of investment to output must increase unless the assumed lag is very large. What is true for a constant rate of growth is *a fortiori* true for any changing positive rate of growth.

9 See note 8.

10 The average share of wages W/Y over the cycle will remain constant, i.e. at the value it would have had in the absence of innovations, if the innovation is neutral not only with respect to the cycle in which it is made but with respect to all subsequent cycles.

Chapter 12

1 The outstanding modern theoretical work on Economic Development

is beyond doubt J. Schumpeter's *Theory of Economic Development,* Harvard Economic Studies, Vol. XLVI. But Schumpeter's work does not lend itself easily to a precise analysis of secular rates of growth of income and other economic variables in which we are interested. Modern Keynesian writings on this topic have been preoccupied with the problem of stagnation and these theories still await statistical verification. Moreover these theories appear to rely heavily on exogenous (or unexplained) phenomena such as the falling rate of population growth and innovation, and therefore do not constitute a complete theory of economic development.

Classical writers were more interested in the problems of economic development than are economists today. There is for instance, to mention only one, the masterly Book II of Malthus' *Principles of Political Economy* on 'The Progress of Wealth' which in clarity and insight has rarely been surpassed. But in spite of this, his, as also his contemporaries' work, while of great help in understanding the general principles involved, is insufficient to add up to a rigorous theory capable for instance of explaining such phenomena as Kondratieff's long waves or the incidence of innovations.

Marx's theory of economic development is not one which many modern economists would accept, partly because of the fallaciousness of individual components of his theory (theory of value, falling rate of profit etc.), partly because they are not prepared to accept his theory of general historical development.

2 It is quite easy to construct models in which there are oscillations in income of constant amplitude about a stationary income level.

3 Innovations must here be understood in the widest sense of any change in the demand or production functions facing producers.

4 'If one can be sure that the system is stable and strongly damped, there is no great harm in neglecting to analyse the exact path from one equilibrium to another, and in taking refuge in a *mutatis mutandis* assumption.' P. Samuelson, *Foundations,* op. cit., p. 331.

5 J.R. Hicks, *The Theory of Wages,* op cit.

6 See M. Kalecki, *Essays in the Theory of Economic Fluctuations,* op. cit., pp. 36 et seq.

7 W.W. Rostow, *British Economy of the Nineteenth Century,* Oxford, 1948, pp. 226–35.

8 John T. Dunlop, *Wage Determination under Trade Unions,* Oxford, Blackwell, 1950, pp. 174–80.

9 Professor Rostow in fact found that 'in general the severity of

competition probably increased between 1873 and 1900', Rostow, *British Economy of the Nineteenth Century*, op. cit., p. 235.

10 Rostow, *British Economy in the Nineteenth Century*, op. cit., p. 229.

Index